Case Studies from Our Time: Musings, Letters and of course, Case Studies
by
The Learned Dr. W.B. Hachenbracht, MD

Printed in Canada

```
        Canadian Cataloguing in Publication Data

Wherley, Jeff, 1968-
   Case studies from our time


   Includes index.
   ISBN 1-55212-373-1


 _I. Title.
PS3573.H4426C37 2000      813'.6      C00-910485-2
```

TRAFFORD

This book was published *on-demand* in cooperation with Trafford Publishing.
On-demand publishing is a unique process and service of making a book available for retail sale to the public taking advantage of on-demand manufacturing and Internet marketing.
On-demand publishing includes promotions, retail sales, manufacturing, order fulfilment, accounting and collecting royalties on behalf of the author.

Suite 6E, 2333 Government St., Victoria, B.C. V8T 4P4, CANADA

Phone	250-383-6864	Toll-free	1-888-232-4444 (Canada & US)
Fax	250-383-6804	E-mail	sales@trafford.com
Web site	www.trafford.com	TRAFFORD PUBLISHING IS A DIVISION OF TRAFFORD HOLDINGS LTD.
Trafford Catalogue #00-0037		www.trafford.com/robots/00-0037.html

10   9   8   7   6   5   4   3   2

"Sanity is statistical."
                                    -George Orwell

For my mother, naturally.

TABLE OF CONTENTS

August 27, 2000

For Grandma,

My most faithful correspondant, who always encouraged me to write and introduced me to Thurber.

Love,

CASE STUDIES

A Case Study from Our Time

Ours, sad to say, is an era of degenerative behavior. Never before has psychosis and violence run so rampantly in our society. The rate for violent deaths is skyrocketing, a child views nearly 4,000 murders on television before he or she turns 10, and yesterday my secretary came up and said, "Hope you have a nice fall," then pushed me down the stairs.

Sociologists have attempted to pin down the cause for such nefarious behavior, but were disqualified for using illegal half-nelsons. So how is the average person going to understand America's frightening trend of escalating violence and aggression? Besides having kids of their own, I mean.

Perhaps through the study of one such warped mentality we may extrapolate to the larger population and come to sympathetically comprehend the labyrinth of violence and psychopathic behavior.

Such a subject is to be found in Fredrick S. Hoosis of Kalamazoo, Michigan. For years, Fred struck terror into the hearts of state residents with his dangerous and disturbed mentality, which has been blamed for everything from his maiming of indigenous wildlife (including his younger brother), to his constant refusal to cover his mouth when he sneezed.

Fred's early case history shows a very natural childhood despite the fact that he reportedly watched television almost constantly. Then he discovered the on/off switch and trouble began to brew.

At age 12, the emergence of his darker side begins to be noted in teacher's report card comments and the occasional piece of graffiti beneath the 12th Street Bridge. During this period, teachers began to complain that Fred was having trouble adjusting socially to his peers: he seemed to be unable to learn their names and referred to all his playmates as, "Hey, you with the face!" Also listed as problematic was his inability to learn the Pledge of Allegiance, choosing instead to hum the theme to *Barney Miller*.

Much of Fred's teen-age years are lost in a blur, due to his principal spilling a cup of Kool-Aide on his file. After his high school graduation, Fred attempted to enter the media and had his first confrontation with the law when he used a crowbar to do so.

He was released under his own recognizance by the courts, but loathed that fact. Years later, Fred was often seen in public attempting to climb on top of his own recognizance.

Meanwhile, Fred's behavior seemed to grow even more frenetic. He spent long hours alternately imitating the criminal activities on his favorite television shows and his mother's cardigan sweater. He once admitted to his guidance counselor (who had never bothered to tell Fred that he had actually graduated and no longer needed to show up for detention) that he would actually be better at imitating his mother's sweater, "If I could only find a hanger that could hold me on the clothes bar."

Frustrated by this lack of success, he became moody and for a brief time took up playing the kazoo in the hope that it would improve his reflexes.

Despite the long hours he spent sitting and playing, Fred was never able to catch more than four quarters off his elbow at once.

While his interest in playing faded, his fascination with sitting seemed to double every day. Fred was completely astounded by the way a couch seemed to be nothing more than three chairs in a row, but three couches in a row seemed to, in his words, "take up too much space."

This seemed to be the turning point for Fred's sanity. Already balancing on the edge of an unhealthy interest in furniture and their relationship with relaxing, he began to place an unusual emphasis on chairs. Fred suddenly found himself surrounded by shady characters who passed themselves off as his "friends" or "Richard Milhouse Nixon". One particularly shady character known as "Stretch" Meadows took Fred aside one day and showed him how he could use the cushions of a couch, a folding chair and an afghan to construct a "fort".

Following this episode, Fred grew even more maniacal about chairs, referring to them by name and apologizing if he broke wind while sitting on them.

Then one night the breaking point came. While sitting in his home watching *Sharky's Machine*, Fred became convinced that one of the dining room chairs was edging closer to him in an attempt to devour his large intestine. Understandably frightened, he jumped up and smashed the chair to pieces on the nearest available object, which turned out to be, unfortunately, his mother.

Fred raced out of the room and into the night, clutching two cushions from the Chesterfield sofa to his body and screaming, "I'm a sandwich, I'm a sandwich!"

Little is known of his activities following this episode, but for months stories circulated of maimed recliners found in vacant lots, and of people who reported seeing a mysterious figure lurking behind their couches when they switched off the light.

While investigating the case, police came across two you boys violating a Lay-Z-Boy behind an abandoned building, one holding the chair down, the other lifting up its lace doilies and chanting, "I see London, I see France..."

When questioned, the boys admitted that they had been given the chair by, "some wacko," and would gladly give his address to the authorities just as soon as they cleared up their rooms a little and could find their Rolodexes.

As it turned out, the police were able to solve the case on an anonymous phone call they received where they were informed, "Someone's been sleeping on my fold-out couch and he's still there!" Arriving on the scene, the police found Fred, although rather than sleeping, he was complaining of the mattress. "It's so thin," he stated in his confession to the police. "You can feel the bar right here in the small of your back."

Promising thicker mattresses, the police were able to lead him away with no difficulties other than sending away an irate pizza delivery driver with the meatball sub Fred had ordered from the woman's apartment.

Seventeen years have passed since Fred began serving time in the state penitentiary. He has made great progress. He is now able to look at a loveseat and coffee table without drooling, and has devoted much of his time to educating children on the Do's and Don'ts of upholstering.

Much has been written about Fred's ordeal and the reign of terror he unleashed, but it is Fred himself who has been credited with the wisest lesson to be learned from his case.

"A lot of people have said maybe I watched too much t.v. when I was a kid," he says. "And other people have said I hung out with the wrong kind of friends. But I prefer to put the blame on the school. They should've seen the warning signs. I mean, if I was at graduation and saw someone trying to eat their diploma, I'd definitely ask if they were feeling o.k."

All Worked Up

"Raul" is a CEO of a large accounting firm. He came to me for anxiety treatment early last year. I immediately identified the source of Raul's problem, but have kept it to myself, as it would only lead to his cure and the end of his treatments with me.

Raul feels a crushing sense of pressure from work. His company handles government contracts, and Raul is obliged to follow many government regulations. This gives him a sense of restriction and loss of freedom.

"They're getting so stringent," he complained to me during our most recent session. "I was walking through the receptionist's area and overheard one telling the other about her activities with her boyfriend over the weekend. I was forced to suspend her for performing oral sex in the workplace because she was talking about it."

The government's 'zero-tolerance' regulations have also affected Raul's business. "We lost an entire workweek last month," he said. "A janitor heard someone say that Rich, one of our top accountants, had been tossing some sharp barbs about in the lobby. He called the police before we could tell him they weren't the type of weapons that did bodily harm.

"The police were forced to haul Rich downtown because state law mandates any response by the police to a phone call reporting potential violence must result in arrest. Unfortunately, the police station is uptown, so there were further delays. By the time we got back, the NRA had scheduled a press conference on our front steps to announce that barbs, especially sharp ones, were the true problem of violence in this country. Protestors had assembled, but they were the wrong ones and kept demanding decriminalization of marijuana laws. They left with seven of my computer programmers for the Hemp-Fest in Wisconsin. When the programmers came back three days later, all they wanted to do was order pizzas and write code for incredibly complex screen-savers. I lost a big account from the Department of Transportation and my toupee because of that week."

Another factor contributing to Raul's stress factor is something he termed, "the explosion of technology in the workplace." I asked him to elaborate on this terminology. "Two computer screens blew up after a power surge last week," he said. "It scared the hell out of me."

But technology has added another dimension of anxiety to Raul's life. "I didn't like the internet at first," he explained. "It seemed overwhelming, just too big and confusing to understand. Then I found out there were pictures of hot, naked women having sex somewhere in cyberspace. Boy-howdy, I started double-clicking with the best of them, pal.

"But since that time, I've felt myself pulled by conflict. I mean, I'm a married man, and I don't think it's hurting that any. In fact, it's given me a few ideas I've brought home and tried out. But I don't like people knowing I do look at them. Which is weird, because every guy I know, when he gets together with another guy, likes to talk about hot, naked women having sex.

"I'd quit doing it, but if I wasn't going to do it, then I'd probably make a policy that everyone in the office couldn't look at internet porn either. And there's a couple of guys on the second floor I'd rather have checking out Racquel Darrian's newest spread than sitting around trying to actually do more than the minimum I've come to expect from them."

I assured Raul this was a perfectly acceptable rationalization.

"But aren't I skipping the larger issues with this compromised thinking," he asked me. "Shouldn't we be digging deeper into the psyche, trying to find the true motives and feelings behind..."

"You want to play some Solitaire on my computer?" I inquired.

"Hey, yeah," he replied. The rest of our session passed very quickly and in almost absolute silence.

Bent Like a Fox

My patient "Bob" remains worrisome to me. He confesses that he may have alcoholic tendencies, but remains unsure.

"Just because my breath is flammable, is that any reason to think that I have a drinking problem?" he lamented during our last session. "What about people who eat Mexican food all the time? Can't they emit noxious fumes as well? Fumes that are capable of bursting into flames?"

"But that's not usually coming from their mouths," I pointed out.

"Oh, sure, take that side," he replied. "It's just like at work. Everyone got mad because I wanted to use the company refrigerator to house a keg of beer. But what about our foooood, everyone whined. All I wanted to do was drill a tap through the door so the keg could be a consistent temperature. And like you need food when you have hops, barley and pure mountain spring water to keep you going.

"But noooo, everyone is upset because then they won't be able to put their lunch in there. What about me? I'm the one running out of beer before noon. Do they think I like making up excuses to get out of the office and down to the Dairy Mart for a beer run?

"People are so selfish. Dave came right up to me and said, 'If you put that keg in, I'll write a memo about it. I bring a bologna sandwich to work every day. If I can't put it in the refrigerator, then it'll taste funny when noon rolls around.'

"I told him that since you are what you eat, it wouldn't do him any harm, because Dave is one of the unfunniest guys I've ever met. He just got mad and left in a huff, which I think is his favorite form of transportation.

"So I called in all the rest of my co-workers and asked them a simple question. I said, 'Which is better, a bologna sandwich, or heaven? The answer seems obvious, because everyone says that nothing is better than heaven. But you also need to consider the fact that a bologna sandwich is better than nothing. So, logically, a bologna sandwich is better than heaven.' Then I hit them all over the head with my electric pencil sharpener. The bastards."

Bob's progress seems evident to me. I only wish more of my patients could see his example.

That's All She Smoked

I lost another patient the other day when Mrs. S stepped outside to smoke a cigarette on a cold evening and couldn't tell when to stop exhaling. She was one of the favorite patients around the office, and the grief of the secretaries is palpable, like a damp Kleenex or perhaps some warm cheese. She was a warm, caring person whose only weakness was for her cigarettes and poking at eyeballs with a sharp stick.

She came to me at the recommendation of her optometrist, who was already wearing one eye patch. I was able to break her of poking habit rather easily. "Imagine if they did it to you," I told her during our first session.

"That would hurt like a bastard!" she exclaimed, and vowed to change her ways immediately. Within a few days she was poking at people's eyes with a pool cue, then moved on to jabbing at their necks with an eight ball. At the time of her demise, she would rarely give in to the urge to rub a piece of green felt on the thigh of a new acquaintance.

Her smoking was another matter. We tried a variety of cessation methods. Mrs. S once went twenty minutes without a cigarette when she took a wrong turn looking for a restroom in my office and locked herself in the janitor's closet. It was her longest abstention.

Mrs. S's history with smoking went back to her very conception. "As I was conceived, my mother was having a cigarette," she confided to me. Mrs. S's mother was a porn star, and the footage she showed me verified her claim.

Mrs. S grew up in the haze of tobacco smoke, which emanated from her hair. Then child-welfare authorities took her away from her mother, preventing her from extinguishing cigarettes on Mrs. S's head. The smoke ceased, but Mrs. S soon took up smoking on her own. She claimed it was not due to peer pressure, but as a coping mechanism. "I needed those cigarettes," she declared during one of our sessions. "They comforted me. Do you know how hard it is be a little kid named Mrs. S? The kids were always laughing at me. Even the teachers would ask where my husband was. So I started smoking to deal with the kids and, later, sleeping with my teacher's husbands to deal with them."

Cigarettes became Mrs. S's constant companion. She learned to eat while smoking, after some initial mistakes ("Filters are actually a good source of fiber," she would laugh). Only sleeping frustrated her. It was impossible for her to continue to extinguish one cigarette and light another without waking up.

She often nodded off with a cigarette in her hand, resulting in a large number of house fires, which she said didn't bother her. "Mattresses give off a large amount of carbon monoxide. It calmed me down while I was hunting for a fire extinguisher." She even wove several comforters out of tobacco leaves to provide additional nicotine. But the rising insurance costs made her search for alternatives.

At first she tried sleeping on a waterbed, which solved the problem of fires, but created annoying flooding in her bedroom. Then she attempted to give up sleep altogether. This worked for nearly two weeks, until she went for a drive one evening and found her car in the Atlantic the following morning. Since she was living in Kansas City at the time, she reconsidered her strategy. In the end, she simply duct-taped a wet pack of cigarettes to her biceps.

She was able to change this practice with the advent of dermatologically-applied nicotine systems. "I love the patch," she declared when I suggested she use it to attempt smoking cessation once again. "If it'd been around when I was a kid, I could've used it to start smoking." Her need for cigarettes had become increasingly strong. Mrs. S had even begun to chew nicotine gum while she smoked. "The heart palpitations tell you it's working," she would gasp between chews.

The changing atmosphere towards smoking began to bother her during the past two decades. "Smoking's bad for you," she once screamed when someone advised her to quit. "What about jogging in Los Angeles? What about drinking bleach? What about driving your car off a cliff? Aren't all those bad for you? And people keep doing that, don't they?" She was less than stable that day.

But the anti-smoking movement only strengthened her resolve. Mrs. S referred to anti-smokers as "Health Nazis" and people who had kicked the habit as "Marty Feldmans". When someone would request her to put out her cigarette, she would reply, "My, it's pouring cats and dogs!" But only when it was raining.

As she had requested, her final wishes will be followed. Her remains have been cremated, placed in an ashtray and shipped off to the R.J. Reynolds Tobacco Corporation. Memorials may be sent to Ernie's Newsstand and Tobacco Shop.

Biodegredation

My patient, "Moon Unit" died the other day, and I still have not adjusted to the loss. How I'm going to meet the boat payments without the money from her counseling sessions is beyond me.

Her name was certainly unique among my patients, and I promised "Moon Unit" that if I ever wrote about her for any published work I would provide a measure of anonymity for her. Thus, the quotation marks.

"Moon Unit" had a second distinction as well in that she was the most radical environmentalist I have ever met. In a way, her death should've been anticipated. Dying was the most earth-friendly thing she could do.

She came to me on the referral of the doctor who served the commune she was living in at the time. I say, "doctor," but he was more of a veterinarian. Actually, he dispensed horse tranquilizers and was pretty good at foot massages. But he was a doctor to "Moon Unit" in that he always billed her for consulting with him and refused to make house calls.

Environmentalism had always been important to "Moon Unit", but it was beginning to shut down her ability to function in the world.

Money was not a factor for her. She had invented a type of granola which took more calories for the body to chew and digest than it provided. It also tasted exactly like a crumbly Hershey's Bar, and the combination proved irresistible. After fighting off a class action lawsuit from several women who had lost nearly all their body weight on an exclusive diet of "Chocanola", "Moon Unit" was set for life.

With her money, she could easily afford a 5th Avenue lifestyle, but "Moon Unit" had been raised by hippies and had a tremendous concern for the environment. She moved to the commune and lived there happily for nearly a year. Then she began to have difficulties, which eventually landed her in my office.

As she told it to me, she became "acutely aware" of the impact her choices could have. Although she didn't quite phrase it that way, choosing instead to scream, "In the name of Mother Earth, I liberate thee!" over and over again while throwing my potted plants out the window.

I will never forget our first session together. She arrived late by nearly a week. She lived more than sixty miles away and had already given up driving. She stood before me, barefoot with beautiful, long hair and said, "It was like, everything, you know?"

To this day, I have no idea what she meant by that, but then she paid me in cash, for three sessions in advance, and that is what stands out in my mind.

As we dug in deeper, past the first thing she said to me, "Moon Unit" began to open herself up to me.

"I always was into taking care of the earth, you know?" she said later on. "It was like, here, and so was I, so I figured, what the hell? I mean, taking care of the earth is like taking care of your dog. Except that you don't have to take the earth on walks or try to figure out how to pick up its droppings in your yard."

Her childhood was typical of an environmentally-friendly family's: camping excursions, household recycling, membership in Greenpeace and the Sierra Club, anonymous bombings of large corporations and other earth-friendly activities filled her days.

When she made her fortune and moved out of her home, "Moon Unit" thought her money would make it very simple for her to live the earth-perfect life she yearned for.

"I thought, man, here's a chance to make everything right, you know? So I bought, like, the best dirt, so we could grow the best vegetables. I bought one of those food dehydrators you see on t.v. because then we wouldn't need to refrigerate anything. Freon's bad for the atmosphere, right? So I don't like refrigerators. And I bought some great Currier and Ives table service so we wouldn't be throwing away any paper plates or anything like that."

But her paradise quickly proved hollow. First of all, she realized the food dehydrator was using electricity, which came from fossil fuels and caused acid rain. She tried the alternative of eating everything cold from a can which she would then recycle, but realized that would mean driving her car to a recycling center or allowing a truck to pick them up, both of which would mean the consumption of more fossil fuels. Then she hit upon the idea of providing year-round fresh fruits and vegetables with a greenhouse she would build, but found the idea morally objectionable.

"You know, it's like those chickens that aren't free range chickens," she told me during a session.

"Not that I'd eat chicken. No way. I mean, think about their souls. Or is it the diseases they carry? My point is, if I was going to eat a chicken, I'd only eat a free range chicken. Eating the other kind is like eating a chicken prisoner, you know? And that's what I thought eating greenhouse veggies would be like. Like eating chicken prisoners. Only vegetables."

At this time, "Moon Unit" found that people in the commune were beginning to bother her on money matters, trying to beg or borrow some portion of her fortune.

"They really bugged me, man," she told me. "I mean, I thought money would be, like, the root of all cool things. That is, like, so not true. I got so tired of trying to keep track of everything. Plus, my accountant, Fredrico? He was just getting too uptight. So I gave almost all of it to the Redwoods. I mean, they are such a nice family. Joe and Helen Redwood, you know them? Totally fun. But they had like, eight kids, and they needed most of that money just for their college funds. So I thought they would be able to use the cash. 'Course, they start using coke and stick most of it up their noses. But it seemed like a good idea at the time."

In the meantime, "Moon Unit's" world continued to collapse around her. Anything involving fossil fuels, killed or imprisoned animals and their by-products, mass-production and potentially-threatening products were taboo for her, and she had little to do but sit in her own filth and card the wool the few sheep on the commune chose to shed.

Too late, she thought of moving to Borneo. But by this time her only option was to swim there and she just didn't have the lungs for it.

In our last session, she talked about how desperate things had become for her.

"I'd like, kill myself, you know?" she lamented. "But I've probably got so many carcinogens from smoking dope and so many preservatives from Taco Bell burritos that it'd take forever before I rotted and then I'd only emit bad things when I did. Jeeze, if there was only some giant place where prehistoric animals had gone to their deaths still around today, I'd probably throw myself into it."

In retrospect, I guess I should've called the La Brea Tar Pits, but I really didn't think she would be able to walk that far, since her diet had been reduced to any fruits or vegetables she found by the side of the road (which qualified them as "free range" to her). And, honestly? I didn't even know the place was still open. I thought they had built a Wendy's over it or something.

Amoral Majorities

"Karl" is a state representative from the Midwest. He came to my office as part of a plea-bargain settlement with a D.C.-area stable buck. While our sessions were brief and numbered only three (although lettered, they went all the way to "V"), I saw issues in "Karl" which are becoming more and more prevalent among politicians.

Karl was ordered to find counseling as part of his agreement with the horse stable from which he had stolen a prime racing stud.

"They say in Washington you should never be caught in bed with a dead woman or a live boy. Well, I've done both and nobody ever blinked an eye." He shrugged at this confession. "It might've helped that they were my first two wives. Finding out Robin was a transvestite was a bit of a shock, but after that, it was no big deal. But just let them find you in bed with a drugged thoroughbred and God Almighty, you'd think you'd tried to shoot the president."

Karl's claim was that he was simply trying to re-enact one of his favorite scenes from *The Godfather* without all the blood. But he ignores the larger issue of having taken something which wasn't his. It is this trend I find disturbing among the public officials I treat.

"Tax money, schmax money," Karl was fond of saying during our sessions. "It's not like it belongs to anybody. Just like that horse I put in my bed...it's all out there anyhow. *Somebody's* got to drug it and sneak it into their hotel room. Or use it to pay for freeways. Or win the Kentucky Derby with it. Why not me?"

Another disturbing tendency I found in Karl, which is also starting to manifest itself in his colleagues, was the fact he had lost touch with his constituents, the very people who had elected him, a fact which he constantly rationalized.

"Hey, in Indiana, we're always slipping horses into beds," he told me during our last session. "It's like a practical joke. I know one guy I went to high school with, when he got married, we slipped a mare into his bedroom on the first night of his honeymoon. Ha! Only trouble was, he never noticed. Kinda nearsighted, Joe was. She wasn't much of a cook, but she could square dance like nobody's business! We figured, long as Joe's happy, why mess with it?"

When I pointed out he was elected to office in Michigan, he changed the subject by eating my potted fern.

Finally, I noticed Karl firmly believed his punishment was far too severe for his crime. He confided to me that he didn't believe he should have to pay any sort of penalty for his "borrowing" of the horse. This, to me, was the most unsettling of Karl's behaviors and the most pervasive among his fellow law-makers. Many seemed to believe they were above the law, or at least had the ability to hover over it briefly. But whenever I tried to get Karl to discuss this, he would inevitably begin talking about his meetings with the officer assigned to handle his probation.

"Jeeze-louise, am I ever getting sick of my parole officer," he would tell me. "For one thing, he's got a face like a pepperoni pizza. I mean, I look at him and all I can think of is Yellowstone Park. I keep wanting to scream, "Get ready laddies, she's gonna blow!" But of course, I can't do that because he'll just write it down in his little book. Never mind that the book is *Where the Wild Things Are*. He scribbles it over Max's face nonetheless, like he's writing a ticket for double parking in front of a fire hydrant. That's really his problem...he's always dreamed of having more authority, like a meter maid has. If I wasn't so close to finishing off my community time, there's no way I'd sit there and let him play, "Good Cop, Bad Driver's Ed Student" with the two swivel chairs in his office. At least it's better than sitting on the couch with Mitch and Tony (who are both on parole after serving a month...they were caught fondling Pepsi © machines in the foyer of the Senate) while he reenacts the last scene from Steinbeck's *The Wayward Bus*. Plus, he stinks whenever the temperature is over fifty outside. I don't know...it's probably some kind of problem with yeast cells or something."

This is the last entry I have from my time with Karl. I am not sure what the solution is, but I hope passing these facts along to the general public will help make people aware of the problem. Perhaps it is time we considered that our system of government may have expanded beyond our founding fathers' original plans, leaving our representatives too cut-off from the places which have elected them. Or maybe we can make national legislative decisions with a specially-designed dartboard. Either way, I'm not voting a straight ticket come November.

Asleep at the wheel and elsewhere

"Ralph" came to me seven years ago for treatment of narcolepsy. His ability to fall asleep was rivaled only by the case study I had read of years ago of one Roger "Bedhead" MacHewson. MacHewson was a junk bondsman in the 1920's who lost his shirt in the Wall Street Crash. His hundreds of thousands of dollars remained untouched in the coffee cans he continually buried in his septic tank, but the shirt, an embroidered Western-style Arrow modeled after General Custer's wedding suit, was torn off him as he raced to find shelter from a sudden storm of plummeting stock brokers. MacHewson was inconsolable and became severely suicidal. However, he didn't get around to taking his life until 1942 because he kept nodding off.

Ralph was a near-second to the legendary MacHewson. Unlike "Bedhead", though, his narcolepsy didn't begin to manifest itself until Ralph's teenage years. Before that, he had known a normal childhood, replete with neighborhood baseball games, familial grooming sessions and glue-sniffing.

The first incident where the narcolepsy occurred was during his freshman year of high school. During a talent show, Ralph was to be the front of a horse costume for a skit several friends had written with the whimsical title *The Horse Was Also From Nantucket* (he told me that although he hadn't contributed to the writing, he had choreographed the dance number by himself).

However, his last memory of what should've been a triumphant exhibition of sophomoric humor was standing in the wings of the stage. He did not regain consciousness for nearly six hours. When he awoke, he found the head of his costume firmly lodged in a pony's rectum. He had no idea how this might have happened, but still was able to find humor in the situation. "You know," he told me after relating this story, "It's kinda ironic when you consider that the horse's head I was wearing ended up..." and then he was asleep. I tucked a blanket around him, slipped him into a large cardboard box and had him U.P.S.'ed back to his apartment.

During our next session, I asked him to mention some of the other situations he had experienced these bouts of narcolepsy.

"When do I fall asleep?" he laughed. "When don't I?

"I've missed classes because of sleeping. I once turned up for a final exam and the professor wouldn't let me take it because I hadn't been there all semester. I once dozed through an encore set at the Rock 'n' Roll hall of fame when Paul, Ringo and George came onstage and began throwing Ecstasy into the crowd and chanting, 'She sells sea shells by the sea shore...buck naked!' Tyra Banks needed to be treated for dehydration after I fell asleep on top of her shortly before we were to consummate the dismissal of her stalking suit against me. She was trapped against the mattress for nearly two days. Whenever a special newscast comes on, I immediately fall asleep, so I've missed out on the space shuttle Challenger's explosion, the war in Iraq, the Berlin Wall's collapse and Reagan's attempted assassination. When Eddy Murray started doing that Buckwheat getting shot on Saturday Night Live, I was like, 'Why is this funny? And couldn't Tim Kazerinsky play Ted Koppel instead of Joe Piscapo?' I never liked him anyhow." He hesitated a moment, then added, "Piscapo, that is. I thought Kazerinsky was hilarious."

I considered his situation carefully, then suggested that perhaps his insomnia was stress-related. "Each time you succumb to your sleeping, you seem to be on the verge of an event or situation which threatens you with uncertainty, if not outright change and all other threats associated with it."

Ralph considered my suggestion carefully, then shook his head. "Not always, though. I think I would've liked my class. It was in geography, which I always enjoyed, and it was called *Topography of Supermodels and other late-20th-century Ubermensch.* Surely that would've been good. And I've fallen asleep while working on my car, masturbating, watching Jell-O wrestling and masturbating in my car. How are those stressful?"

"All have uncertain outcomes," I told him, shaking my head as well. "You didn't know how you would do in the class. And would you successfully repair your car, reach climax, identify the winner of the pugilistic bout and avoid staining your bucket seats?"

"How did you know I have bucket seats?"

I shook Ralph's head for him. "Unimportant. What is important is that you are subconsciously avoiding the tension of an unresolved situation by sleeping through the struggle and awakening when all has been decided."

Ralph shook all over. "No way. I go to Vegas all the time and play the pony races in Atlantic City. I never fall asleep there and that's where I make most of my money as well as get my knees broken."

"But perhaps your confidence in the matter allays your narcolepsy. Or perhaps it is simply adrenaline, the importance of the moment keeping you awake?"

"I fell asleep skydiving one time. That should've been an adrenaline-charged moment instead of a six-month intensive-care stint," he replied, shaking his hips.

"Again, it might be a matter of priorities, or simply it was overstimulation and your brain was merely seeking a release."

"Yeah, but I..." Ralph began, shaking my groove thang, which I had forgotten to put away when I came back from lunch.

"Oh, to hell with it," I said, and gave him a prescription for a bottle of amphetamines.

Land's End

"Juan" is a wealthy suburbanite who was referred to me recently. He sought help after a breakdown in his belief system. That, and the court-ordered psychiatric counseling. But we'll come to that shortly.

Juan worked as a real estate salesman for more than thirty years after spending brief stints as a stock boy, cooper, ombudsman for Fredrick's of Hollywood, border-crossing drug mule, clergyman and rodeo clown.

Juan told me in our initial session he enjoyed his work as a cooper tremendously, but when he discovered that his labors were contributing to the production of barrels, he quit as a conscientious objector.

The rest of his labors were to make money, he admitted. The tax-free life of priesthood appealed to him, but when he awoke from a drunken gambling binge in Atlantic City to find himself married, he had to give it up.

Real estate was where Juan found his niche. "They say, 'Location, location and location are the three keys to selling real estate," he told me. "Early on, I got this property on the lake, four bedrooms, three baths, a two car garage and a boathouse with a forty foot dock. That's where I made my money. 'Cause I sold it at least fifteen times. So they built it on some kind of Native American grave site. So sue me. Was that my problem? A tree eats your kid and you want to blame the REMAX guy? C'mon."

But as the years passed, Juan began to find more and more time on his hands. His children grown, his business becoming regular and less time-consuming, he looked about for something to fill the void.

He found yard work. It was the beginning of the end.

Juan had always prided himself on a well-kept lawn, but now with money and time at his disposal, he began to push it.

He described his initial experiment to me over a cup of coffee and under a bagel with pear butter, which I keep suspended from my office ceiling. The tragedy started out innocently enough.

"I started out with just a push mower and a riding mower, plus a weed-eater, you know, just to trim around the garage," he told me. "Then one day I thought, 'Could I get any closer to the sidewalk here? Do something to make the line sharper?' And you know what? I could. It wasn't a week later that I was in the hardware store and I found an edger. I took it home and suddenly realized I had a sharper line on my sidewalk than my neighbor did.

"I was elated. Being in real estate, I knew how important appearance was to property value. My lines were so sharp along the edge of my sidewalk. No grass pushing up against the cement, no dirt lapping on the whiteness of the concrete. Just, whap! Grass stops, sidewalk begins! Ha! I was on top of the world! I couldn't stop thinking about it, it was just a great feeling.

"I don't know if you've ever edged a lawn, Doc, but the line doesn't stay there for long. Five days, maybe a week, and then...." He trailed off and absently-mindedly solved the word jumble I had saved from my Happy Meal. "Hell, it's like you used a weed-eater in the first place, or even," he stifled a sob, "Just ran a friggin' trowel up the edge. You know? You have to keep after it. And it's like the lawn adjusts to the work. Soon, it's less than a week, then it's four days and then three. I mean, what the hell is it with grass? How does it know to grow where you don't want it?

"So I have to adjust. If my lawn needs me out there twice a week, three times, I'll do it. I mean, heck, what's the difference, right? I've got the time, I've got the money to pay for the gas and oil, it keeps the house property up there and it's that much less time I have to listen to my wife tell me what her friends' kids are doing with their kids. I mean, win-win, all the way around right?

"Except that while I'm out there, I suddenly start realizing that the grass I'm trimming back isn't consistent. Oh, consistent. That's what you want from your lawn. You know, Doc, like the outfield at the Ballpark in Arlington, or the infield at the Indianapolis 500. But that's not what I've got. Some places thick, other places thin, grass is different colors in different places and I realize I haven't had the thing re-seeded since I've lived there.

"Sure, I checked for weeds and sprayed for them and felt a crushing sense of shame if a dandelion sprouted on my tree lawn. But what good American doesn't?

"So I've got to get a consistent lawn. I call this lawn service and they come to spray the lawn. It's supposed to even out the acidic level of the soil, up the pH, that sort of thing.

"They hit me, and suddenly it's a miracle. Wham! Green. Oh, my God, how much green! It springs up overnight! But it doesn't last. It starts to slow down, the lawn regresses. Within a week it's like not only is it not only not growing greener, but I swear I can see the weeds starting to make progress.

"So I call them up and ask them to hit me again. But they can't fit me into their schedule. And they also say that they try to keep people on a rotation, not spray their lawn too often.

"I hang up and try to put it out of my mind. But by now I'm seeing weeds everywhere! Everywhere, Doc! My wife, she says our lawn is fine. But what the hell does she know? Has she ever mowed the freakin' lawn once in her freakin' life? She wouldn't know fescue from Kentucky Blue if it came up and bit her on the leg.

"I know our lawn needs help, and I know there's only one thing to do. I slip down to the study later that night and call another lawn service. Get their answering machine and leave a message.

"The next day they come out and hit my lawn. And I start getting the green again. Only this time it doesn't seem to happen overnight. Takes longer and that makes me antsy. So I call the first service again and they say they can fit me in after about three days. So I say, "Go ahead," and schedule them. But I end up calling another place in the meantime, and they hit me while I'm waiting. By August, I had five different lawn care services hitting my house on a regular basis. But I've got the best lawn on the block.

"I've found if you want the best lawn, you've got to have the equipment for it. So I went out and got the stuff. Not all at once, but it just started sneaking up on me. First I got an aerator, then a root zone injection system. Gotta have good circulation to the roots, you know.

"Then the accessory stuff, hedge trimmers, rototiller, weed sprayer and that sort of stuff.

"The summer was pretty dry and some leaves would come down after storms, so I picked up a blower, gas-powered, hand-held. But it wasn't getting everything off my lawn. So I picked up one of those lawn-sweeping units with a chipper and bagging system built into it."

Juan admits he might have begun to overspend at this point, but he remained in a state of denial. During one of our sessions, he stated, "I guess that was when I felt the first twinge, after I bought the sweeper unit. I was running it one evening after some leaves had come down, and suddenly it occurred to me that I was vacuuming my *lawn*. But I put that thought out of my head. After all, that thought wasn't going to pick up the leaves for me, was it?"

However, Juan began to expand his lawn-tending duties. He rationalized it by saying that real estate values were dependant on the type of neighborhood a house stood in.

At first his excursions were innocuous enough, running his mower a few feet over his property lines, fertilizing an elderly neighbor's lawn.

But soon Juan began to lose control. He found himself slipping out of the office early in the afternoon so that he would be able to clandestinely edge his neighbor's driveway. He began to modify his equipment so it would make as little noise as possible.

During one block party, he managed to mow seven lawns on his street by pretending to chase a very slow-moving moth with his riding mower. He would slip out at night to trim the bushes on all the houses across the street.

Eventually Juan was caught in the act when, in the dim light of early morning, he navigated his aerator into a neighbor's swimming pool. At the time of his arrest for trespass and willful over-watering, police found an astonishing stash in Juan's garage, including 350 feet of garden hose, a cement-casting lab capable of turning out at least seven concrete geese in a 24-hour period and nearly half a mile of heavy-duty extension cords.

With this evidence, the picture looked grim: Juan was facing suspension of his riding tractor's license for up to a year and a probationary period of seven years including thorough testing for all drugs, including herbicides and fertilizers. The judge was merciful, however, and recommended Juan see me for counseling.

Juan has made great progress in our sessions. He can now stare at a patch of Astroturf for more than five minutes without bursting into tears, and has quit trying to rearrange the small patch of poison ivy growing outside my window (a fortunate thing, as we are four stories up and the ledge is really quite narrow). Perhaps one day he may be able to run a weed-whacker with the same nonchalance a normal man would use. Until then, he will have to make do with the round-tipped scissors I have provided for him.

Have None, Won't Travel

"Dave" is one of the worst xenophobes I have encountered in my many years of practice. His constant state of denial has made treatment very difficult.

He is an excellent rationalizer, and for the longest period of time was able to keep me from seeing the true source of his problems. I initially put him down as a neurotic, then complemented him as a neurasthenic before finally recognizing his fear of unfamiliar cultures.

"Dave" says categorizing him as a xenophobe is neither fair nor accurate of me; he claims that my unfulfilled desire to experience the glamour of world travel (I admit to having mentioned my longing to see Istanbul and Cincinnati during our sessions) has made me project this conclusion upon him. Perhaps he is right.

But in the meantime, I am unable to find any other reasonable explanation for his behavior. Dave has changed careers, relationships and even his way of life, and there is only one reasonable explanation that I can find: his overwhelming fear of foreign cultures.

Some very simple examples leap readily to mind: despite having labored for years on voice lessons, Dave immediately renounced his dream of being an internationally-renowned opera baritone when he learned he would have to leave Buffalo, N.Y.; even though it went against his strict Catholic upbringing and brought scorn from his parents and letter bombs from his grandmother, he sued for divorce when he learned his wife Cicciolina Cussamano was actually descended from Italian heritage and wished to visit Italy on occasion to see her grandparents; Dave has recently ceased one of his favorite activities – crossing the border to Canada to take advantage of the currency exchange rate and saying, "Beauty, eh?" to anyone with Ontario license plates.

During a recent session, I quizzed him about this change. He became defensive, first pretending he hadn't heard me, then acting as though I had asked him how to play Monopoly.

Once I had broken down these barriers with a Louisville Slugger, Dave became much more willing to talk. He admitted that while the exchange rate was better than ever, and he still giggled whenever he ended a sentence with "eh," he could no longer tolerate the bilingual merchandise he so often had to purchase in Canada.

"It's like it's written in English, *and* in French," he exclaimed during a session.

"It's not like that," I rejoined, "It is."

He glowered darkly for a few seconds, attempted to glower brightly, then gave it up and moved on.

"I mean, I get a bag of Lay's Salt 'n' Vinegar Potato Chips ® the last time I'm up there. Lay's Potato Chips ®! What's more American than that? But there, underneath the usual spiel you always see on a bag of chips, there's the whole thing in French."

He paused, then coughed. I remained silent. I could tell he was nervous by the way he had wet himself. I tried to lighten the mood by juggling some vacuum cleaners.

He lit a cigarette, then ground it into the pile carpeting in my office. Then he lit a cigar, ran out to the parking lot and threw it into my Mercedes' glove compartment. When he returned, I knew he was ready to continue.

"The thing is," he continued, "It makes me nervous.

"I mean, I don't know a lick of French. I can look up at the English part and try to guess it, but no matter what, it sounds threatening to me. I don't think I'm that far off, doc. I think it's a threat.

"I mean, on the chip bag, it's got their little slogan in capitals: BETCHA CAN'T EAT JUST ONE! Nothin' wrong with that, right? Just a friendly little slogan, right?

"But there's some stuff under that, in French, in caps, and I gotta tell ya," here he paused and shook like a well-trained standard poodle.

"Tell me what," I inquired as I withdrew my hand from his.

"It says…" he took a deep breath, which I had placed on top of my desk in anticipation of this moment, swallowed it, and continued. "It says, *'GAGEONS QUE VOUS NE POURREZ PLUS VOUS ARRETER!'* That doesn't sound like a slogan to me. It sounds like someone's plannin' to dish out some pain!"

"I'm not sure I follow you," I said, as I followed Dave into my private bathroom. "Tell me more."

"Tell you?" He pressed his teeth against the commode tank to indicate the futility of such a command. "I mean, sound it out, man. Sound it out!

Gageons. Gageons? Gagons? Gogons? If you ask me, I think it's way too close to 'gargoyles' (which we all know the French created) to be a mere coincidence.

"Then the rest of it falls into place. Que vous is a verb form, we all know that. Like the verb 'be' in English. Plus, 'vous' sounds like 'vex' to me, especially when you say it out loud. And we all know that 'plus' means 'and'. The other stuff you can sound out: porrez? Poporri. Arreter? Arrest.

"So now the sentence shapes up like this: 'Gargoyles will vex you with pouporri, and then arrest you!' Is this the message you want your potato chips to have?"

He shook his head, then shook my hand again. "And *huile vegetale*. What the hell is that? Huge vegetables? All I can say is that this whole Nutella thing scares the hell out of me."

The Fix Is Off

The modern world threatens us with a myriad of technological puzzles. More and more of the everyday items we use are of a high-technology caliber.

Computers are commonplace, yet few people can do much more than double-click the mouse in event of trouble. It is the rare man who can repair a telephone. And what about that funny buzzing noise you keep hearing when you turn your alarm clock off in the morning? Do you think that's just going to go away if you ignore it? Forget it, buster. It's only going to get worse before it gets better.

While computerized machines are incredibly complex, other parts of the typical American lifestyle aren't far behind. Few homeowners these days can repair their own toilets, fewer still adjust the fuel intake of their furnaces. And if you think you can do something about the way the kitchen light sputters, you're just kidding yourself.

Small wonder, then, that people are becoming increasingly frustrated with their inability to deal with the world of machinery, which we accept as commonplace.

But until I met "Bob," I had never met someone who exhibited such anxiety on the subject. His internalization of fear of mechanized objects had reached a delusional stage by the time he came to my office.

The triggering effect had apparently been a string of poor relationships with repairmen and contractors. They all kept dying while attempting to perform various repairs on his college apartment. One had fallen off his roof to his death. This might have been unremarkable, barring the fact Bob lived in a ranch house and the man had taken the tumble seventeen times, according to the coroner's report. One had tried to track down a faulty wire that apparently had lead him headfirst into a Chicago landfill.

The latest victim had been a general contractor who had been found in Bob's apartment, facedown in a container of sour cream with a Shetland pony strapped to his back. The doctor's verdict had been a heart attack. Bob confessed to me that he was feeling suspicious.

"I don't know, Doc," he told me. "I think, maybe, someone doesn't want those repairs to get done. And who could it be but my landlady?"

Bob related to me that his relationship with his landlady, Poppy, was more than a little strained. When he signed the lease, it had included a no-pet clause in it. Less than two weeks after moving in, she caught him with his hand up a date's sweater. She alluded to his impropriety when he dropped by to pay his monthly rent by kneeing him in the groin.

Since that time, relations between Bob and Poppy had deteriorated at a rate matched only by Bob's apartment. When he reported a leaky sink to her, she told him it was only a malfunctioning telegraph in the junk drawer. When passing vandals broke a window, Poppy insisted Bob had fabricated the story. She gave him the choice of paying for the new pane of glass or wrapping enough layers of

Reynolds's Wrap around a sheet of cardboard to obtain an R-13 insulation rating. Bob eventually paid the bill in whole, but this was unacceptable to Poppy, who wanted it paid in either cash or a personal check.

Bob's patience had been pushed to the breaking point when he discovered his water heater was actually a foul-tempered Irishman whom Poppy would taunt in order to raise the water a few degrees. He hired a contractor who promised to not only rid Bob's basement of the Irishman, but to heat his water to a degree Bob would find comfortable enough to keep him from sinking into a tight, shrieking fetal position each time he entered the shower.

But the plumber was discovered choked to death on a length of his own hose and the Irishman began helping himself to any liquor in Bob's apartment.

A pattern began to emerge: Bob's apartment would present some new difficulty which he would promptly report to Poppy, who would pretend she hadn't heard by sticking Roman candles into her ears. Bob would then try to hire a contractor to take on the work, and they would either disappear or die before the job could be completed.

I inquired why Bob hadn't felt it behooved him to make a personal effort to succor his domestic maladies.

"What?" he replied.

"Why didn't you fix the damn thing yourself," I snapped.

He shrugged. "I'm just no good at that sort of thing. I get it from my father. He would never try and fix something on his own. He'd always either have someone come to the house to fix whatever was wrong, or we'd move."

"So he wasn't handy?"

"Actually, he wasn't bad at that sort of thing. He just never had time for it. He was always bringing his work home with him. He was a workaholic. It destroyed our family."

I shook my head gently. "Come now, you're exaggerating. Many men find it necessary to complete tasks at home. It doesn't have to be a negative thing."

"It was for us," Bob insisted. "My father was a demolition expert. He was always experimenting with explosives in the garage. One night he was out there and suddenly, he was gone. So was the garage. They eventually found him in a parking lot, a corn field and several treetops."

Given this bit of history, I could now understand Bob's reluctance to undertake repairs on his own. But how to make him understand the deaths of the repairmen had been nothing more than a morbid coincidence? Or were they? I suddenly lit upon an idea, which was next to the beanbag chair in which Bob was sprawled.

I outlined my plan to Bob, who readily agreed to try it. It would prove conclusively exactly what tie, if any, there was between the deaths of the repairmen and Poppy.

Two Thursdays later, Bob nonchalantly painted a recreation of Monet's "Water Lilies" on his toilet tank, then left his apartment to take his dog for a walk.

He called me at three a.m. that Friday. "It's worse than you think," he said, his voice nearly unrecognizable with anxiety and what sounded like seventeen Altoids. "You'll see in the paper today."

I scanned the early edition with great anxiety, then found the item I was searching for. Underneath the "Police Complaints" column, among the listings of scratched cars and stolen lawn ornaments, was the following: *at 11:36 p.m., a resident of 118 Denmore Avenue reported he had returned from taking his dog for a walk to find his living room, valued at $4,000, had been redecorated and the dog stolen.*

Bob never returned to counseling with me. But I heard he had moved to a southern state, and was living in a rent-controlled tent. I sent him a few sheets of tarpaulin and my best wishes in care of general delivery. I don't know if he received it, but I do know one thing. Both Bob and myself are sleeping better these days.

Rosa's Man

"Rosa Carlotta" is a classic study in gender anxieties and sexual transference. Take, for example, the dream she tells me she always has after a date: she is frolicking in a sunlit field of flowers, laughing because she had just been undercharged for her grocery bill, when she hears the sound of someone else's laughter. She looks up to see an incredibly handsome man dashing towards her, a loaf of Wonderbread in one hand, a bottle of Mad Dog in the other.

"A loaf of bread, a jug of wine and thou," he shouts. "And what a good price besides!"

She halts, unsure of her feelings towards him now. Is it truly love? Or is it simply an animal impulse, as she had once felt towards her cat after an evening of illicit drug use? Rosa calls to the man, "Prove that you love me."

"Oh Rosa, I want only to make you happy," he replies. She laughs and turns into a hedgehog, realizing no man, no matter how sensitive, would say that unless he had been reading the magazines on her coffee table. Rosa then runs away with a second hedgehog who pulls up next to her in an expensive car and announces, "Hey baby, I'm pre-med. Heh-heh-heh."

This dream truly puzzled her. "What does it mean?" she would ask me during our sessions. I asked her what she thought it meant. She had several ideas – perhaps she was afraid to trust someone? Or should she simply rely more upon her instinctive feelings? Or should she stop munching on sauerkraut before she went to bed?

I complemented Rosa on her thoughts on the subject. Of course, anyone with a Ph.D. would know they were all wrong. Rosa was obviously in transition, as represented by the image of the hedgehog in her dream, moving from a stereotypical paradigm of relationships to a more personal one. This was reiterated in the following thoughts Rosa shared with me.

She said she often found herself wishing she were of Italian descent, a race known for its passionate women. "Just look at me," she complained while practicing the hula on my couch. "My eyes are large and brown, my skin is the color of a ripening olive, my hair is dark and thick, and I can't believe how large my..."

Suddenly it struck her that she was Italian, and had always wished she were a Muslim because it would be much easier to pick out an outfit.

"Do you think that would make a big difference in your life," I inquired, quietly filing my nails under "N".

"I don't know," she said, giving her hips a final shake that would've melted most television censors into a pile of sobbing hormones. "Probably not. Maybe it's the men I keep picking."

I urged her to tell me of a typical date. Coincidentally, she had been on one just the previous night.

The evening, she told me, had been pretty routine: flowers, dinner, dancing and sex. The trouble was, Rosa reflected, her dates always seemed to start out with sex and then lead on to the other things. Just once, she would like to begin her evening with flowers, or dinner, or even flowers for dinner.

Not that she disliked sex. It was just that starting out with it seemed to put a strain on the men she was with. Last night had been a prime example. She could tell somehow her date was uncomfortable in the way he avoided eye contact, the way he jumped from topic to topic, the ski mask he had worn throughout the remainder of the evening.

Perhaps it was that she had been too straightforward at the start. Rosa remembered the first man she had bared herself to. In the middle of dinner she had leaned forward and confessed, "I want to be desired, I want you to ravish me so I know you want me." After the headwaiter had performed the Heimlich maneuver on her date, he had spent the rest of the night trying to avoid her, first by involving himself in a game of darts, then, when that failed, by posing as a hat rack

"Are my expectations too high," she asked me during our twenty-seventh session. I could tell that she was nearing a breakthrough by the way she had chosen to wear a Wonderbra for that day's session. I asked her just what kind of expectations she had for men.

"I think my parents were very materialistic, and they burned that thought into my mind," she replied. She could remember how her mother had always encouraged her to find a man who could support her. "Look at our plumber," her mother would tell her as he crouched beneath their sink in his sagging pants. "He is not much to look at, granted, but good lord in heaven, does he pull in the cash."

Once, in a fit of enthusiasm, Rosa's mother had actually tried to get the plumber to take her away by dressing her up as a clogged valve, but the plumber had seen through the ploy when he tried to use a roto-rooter on her and she had flinched.

Perhaps some of her problems also came from her father. He had steadfastly kept her away from males while she was growing up, and then had suddenly thrust her into the company of men whom he expected her to marry.

"What is wrong with this young man?" she remembered him saying. "So he's only eight years old. Big deal, you're what, twelve? You'll grow into it."

The trouble was, she had been twenty-three at the time. Her father could never remember a birthday.

"Yesss, yesss," I muttered as she related these memories. "Classical overtones of an Oedipal complex, merged with familial issues, naturally, and conflict on materialism."

"So what should I do? I mean, I've gone over this a hundred times in my head, talked it all over with you, and I just don't know what my next step is," she said, blinking back tears of desperation.

"Well," I shrugged. "We are by no means near resolution. Your therapy is just beginning. Unless, of course, you want to have sex with a father figure who could provide a gestalt effect for your emotions. Say, a psychiatrist you've been in treatment with? Hey? Get jiggy with Big Doctor Daddy?"

But I already knew she wouldn't. What is wrong with these young people today that they don't want to do things the easy way?

Up and Not Dirty

"Winnie" is a longstanding patient whom I have repeatedly urged to sit, or at least lean against a doorway. The most interesting part of Winnie, though, is that she is a famous talk-show host. And as many Hollywood psychiatrists can tell you, famous people usually have more money than nonfamous people do. This explains why I have had so many more sessions with Winnie than many of my other patients.

To be truthful, she had some issues before she became famous. For example, the tabloids have often run many stories on the "drinking problem" Winnie supposedly overcame to gain her fame. Nothing could be further from the truth. Winnie didn't have the slightest problem with drinking. As a matter of fact, she was incredibly good at it. So much so that she woke up in the middle of her second marriage with no recollection of the first.

She left the bottle behind her as she began her career. But during the first blush of her success, she went on a tremendous bender that resulted in the tragic resurgence of bell-bottomed pants.

I urged her to seek treatment at the Betty Ford center, which she did most successfully. The experience so impressed her that she would often remark to me, "If I ever have enough money, I'd like to build a place where Betty could pop pills. Then she could really experience how special her place is by having treatment there herself."

Since that time, Winnie has been clean and sober. She channels her energies into philanthropic activities, raising money for the rainforest, whales, owls, dolphins, PETA, the humane society...for just about anything other than humans. When I pointed this out to her, she shrugged. "Animals can't hold telethons," she told me. "Doesn't it seem human-centric and selfish to be all like, ooh, let's cure cancer in *people*, and let's get rid of AIDS in *people*, and let's do this for *people* and that for *people*? Aren't animals people too?"

I told her whether or not animals were people was not the point. "The point is, Winnie, you are making tons of money, and yet you are doing nothing questionable with it. People like a little bit of dirt on their celebrities. Hell, if they eventually clean up, people love a lot of dirt on their celebrities. Look at Hugh Grant and Robert Downey, Jr. Completely different problems, but they've made amends and are better-known than ever. Or even if they don't clean up, it can still be a career-booster. Look at Jimi Hendrix. As popular as ever three decades later. You need something. Anything's a problem nowadays. Shopping addiction. Fear of public toilets. Anorexia. Anything."

Try as I would, Winnie remains committed solely to her altruistic programs. However, she more than compensates for her philanthropic ways with a healthy sense of ego. She spends a great deal of time bragging about the scope of her influence.

Winnie used to keep fan mail in her purse. "Never know when you might need to start a fire," she would tell me. "Do you know how many people buy books because I tell them to, or go to a movie because I tell them I liked it? People just listen to me. It's easier than thinking. I got a letter from a woman. She watched my show about how many actresses got famous after getting breast implants, so she got a pair. Then I did a show about the potential dangers of breast implants, and she had them taken out. Then I did a show about how men found breast implants incredibly sexy, and she was confused, so she only had one put in. I did a show about her and got more than a hundred irate letters from men whose wives or girlfriends had just gotten one boob done."

During our last session, I asked her if she found this sort of power frightening in any way.

"Oh, no," she assured me. "I'm a person whose had to fight her weight, the bottle and put a helluva lot of skeletons waaay back in the closet. If you think I don't enjoy screwing with other people's lives, you've got another thing coming."

I think perhaps we have stumbled upon a vice after all. I await our next session with anticipation.

Letters

Bronx Stabbing Ruled Fan Interference

Dear Dad,

I thought you might be interested in the clipping I have enclosed below. I know that you usually don't take much interest in the cases I handle, but I am guessing that the sports-related theme of this particular case might have already brought some of the essential facts to your attention.

This clipping is from *USA Today.* I hope you won't construe my use of this periodical as an endorsement of it. It's simply that since you dropped out of school after the sixth grade to pan for gold in the backyard, I thought it might be more accessible for you.

As you will notice, I was the key witness for the defense. The defense in this case, I should clarify, consisted of several highly-paid lawyers, rather than a blitz formation or having the outfield shifted to the left.

I hope you enjoy this article. I always enjoy sports-related matters. They seem to be the glue that holds our father-son relationship together. I remember the last time we were at a baseball game together. The catcher had just hit a two-out homer with a full count on him, and you turned to me and said, "Jesus H., can't you get down here more often than every other inning? Some of us get thirsty in the bleachers, too!" But after I told you that you could buy more than one beer at a time, we got along just fine, and the other concessionaires thought it was really funny when you started throwing peanuts at me in the seventh inning.

But that was back when I was working summer jobs to get me through grad school and you were contemplating a sex change. It seems like yesterday, really, especially when I run across the odd piece of lingerie in the garage when I'm home. Here's the piece:

Bronx Stabbing Death Ruled "Fan Interference".

BRONX, NY – A New York Court ruling has acquitted Joe Argolissa of all charges in the death of Cleveland Indians left fielder Richie Sexson last Thursday.

Argolissa was released from custody Friday morning when the judge accepted the jury's verdict of not guilty. Argolissa's defense argued the charges were preposterous, and the incident was merely one of fan interference.

The matter started when Sexson, a backup left-fielder for Cleveland, chased a foul ball hit by Tino Martinez during last week's game between the Yankees and Indians.

Martinez's foul ball went into the first row of seats in shallow left field. Sexson, who is 6'8" tall, leaned into the seats.

Argolissa, sitting in the first row, contested Sexson for the ball by first blocking him with his body, then producing a switchblade knife, which he plunged into Sexson's back, just below Richie's right shoulder blade.

Sexson was taken to a local hospital, where he later died of a collapsed lung and shock.

Hospital administrators said the death was not unusual in this situation. "We often see this sort of case here in the Bronx," Sue Brenley, admissions administrator, said in a statement to police. "Sexson's body was traumatized by the loss of the lung, and the shock came when a nurse continuously stuck him with a cattle prod after he refused to give her an autograph by remaining unconscious."

Argolissa, a native New Yorker, is described by his attorneys as "a devout Yankees fan and a real Mafioso-type, brutal and nearly psychopathic, who dotes on his wife and two little girls."

The defense called upon Dr. W.B. Hachenbracht as their key witness.

Hachenbracht, a noted psychiatrist and late-night television spokesman for a variety of products, argued that Argolissa's actions were merely fan interference, induced by professional baseball's base marketing.

"Mr. Argolissa is merely acting upon the urgings of the very league he has paid money to for the privilege, privilege, mind you, of watching men who make ten, even twenty thousand dollars more than he does," Hachenbracht told the jury.

"Argolissa has spent his entire lifetime as a Yankees fan, and what has he received in return? Several World Series Championships, true, but outside of that, what?

"He has purchased hats, T-shirts, coats and many other objects which have given revenue to his beloved organization. And one time, just one time, he goes to get something back from this game, from this organization, from this team, his team, and he becomes the enemy," Hachenbracht argued.

The doctor went on to explain the phenomenon known as BIRGING, or Basking In Reflected Glory. In this situation, fans of a team try to make a team's success their success.

"Argolissa has simply taken it one step further," Hachenbracht stated. "Rather than just talk about his team, he has attempted to help his team by keeping an opposing player from making a play on the ball, and killing him in the process."

The jury moved unanimously for acquittal, and the judge concurred. "Mr. Argolissa, I would like to apologize to you on behalf of the entire court system," Judge Richard Price said after hearing the jury's decision. "We have wasted your time and ours with this unseemly peep show."

With the ruling of fan interference, Martinez's ball is considered an automatic out, rather than a dropped foul ball. Accordingly, his homerun later in that inning will be ruled invalid, and the Yankees' win will be only 5 to 3, rather than 6 to 3.

Argolissa withheld comment until the court was out of session. As he entered his limousine, he made a brief statement to the assembled press corps, saying he would be filing suit for harassment, cruel and unusual punishment and "whatever else those suits I pay so much money to can think up."

Argolissa then added that the press could, "get the fuck out of his way," or he'd give them "the Sexson treatment".

Well, I hope you enjoyed this. I know you're always looking out for sports memorabilia, and I've talked with the medic who cut Sexson's jersey off on the way to the hospital. If I can get it for you, I'll let you know. Talk to you later.

Your son,
Dr. W.B. Hachenbracht

You Think that's a Big Deal, Huh?

Dear Dr. Horowitz[1],

My patient "Juliet" is testing my limits. Her use of sarcasm has spiraled into an ever-deepening mire of relentless abuse and misunderstandings. I have tried to stay objective during our sessions, but I find myself becoming defensive, forgetting that Juliet has no other way to express herself.

Juliet began using sarcasm at an appallingly young age. She discovered it as a defense mechanism at the age of seven while she lagged behind in growth spurts. Other children were able to run faster, jump higher and so on. Juliet began to develop an edge, which can only be described as acerbic. With a withering look of scorn, she would stand at the start line of a track race and say, "Why should I follow them when they're just going to run back to me anyhow?"

When she realized that friends were laughing at her remarks, she began to use it on a daily basis. This led to the use of sarcasm in order to be accepted in social situations. From that point, it was a short step to using it on a daily basis to make a statement or simply highlight the meaninglessness of daily human existence.

Eventually she reached a point where she couldn't communicate without sarcasm, no matter

---

[1] Dr. Horowitz was an associate of Dr. Hachenbracht who annoyed Dr. H. to no end. He was, however, an incredibly good partner in games of "charades".

how intimate the situation. I accompanied Juliet to a Marriage Encounter retreat one time, an event that sticks in my head like so much bubble gum in a mustache. The couples were asked to list at least one virtue their spouse had. After her husband had stood and run off a nearly interminable list of her virtues, Juliet stood and said, "My husband is, if nothing else, a fantastic lover. The other night he was banging at me so long, the dog started barking at the bed, thinking an Avon Lady was trying to get into the house."

She came to me on her own. I will give her that much...plus bus fare, if she wants it. I guess I am trying to express how frustrated I am in trying to reach her.

Our first session is a good indication of how things have been going. Juliet's first words to me were, "Oh, so you're the great doctor I'm supposed to see. Well, maybe you can work the big miracle everyone's been hoping for. My friends say I use too much sarcasm. I say their butts would be smaller if they used their heads more, instead. Mandy is so scared that her wittle boy is going to grow up that she hasn't let him buy his own clothes yet, and the poor thing's nearly into middle school. But his classmates won't eat him alive, oh no! 'Cause he's got moxie. That's what his mother says...he's got moxie. Oh yeah, moxie counts for a helluva lot in today's world." My attempts to reach Juliet in subsequent sessions have not been much more conducive.

I once suggested that we try a relaxation technique. "Oh, a relaxation. That's gonna help me," she replied. "Just sit back and act like you don't have any troubles. That's why you're at the psychiatrist's office to begin with, isn't it?"

I just about punched her. But I refrained, held back at the last moment by the knowledge that the Hippocratic Oath I held sacred demanded my self-control, and that she had not yet written a check for this session.

If you have any input for this case, I am very anxious to hear it. Juliet is driving me nuts, and I have nearly forty more cases exactly like her.

Sincerely,

Dr. W.B. Hachenbracht.

A Proper Prescription

"Earl" is a claims processor/verifier for a large health insurance company. He was recommended to me after he wrote the following letter in response to a customer's complaints:

Dear Mr. Getty,

Your letter was received by my company and forwarded down the line of command like a hot potato until it ended up on my desk.

Your complaints, as I understand them, are that you find it unfair that you should have to pay more for a name-brand pharmaceutical prescription than a generic one, and that you are enraged by the fact that this insurance company contacted your doctor to inquire whether or not a generic alternative would be acceptable for your prescription. Let me answer you inquiries in reverse order.

I'm sorry that you find it terrible that our insurance company would have consulted with your doctor and changed your prescription

without consulting you. But that's
what insurance companies do these
days. You sacrifice a small amount
of your privacy in return for having
nearly every malady paid for by this
company. It's pretty much par for
the course. Ask around.

As far as having a generic
substituted for a brand name
prescription, let me assure you that
there is not one goddam bit of
difference between them. My wife
has worked in a pharmacy for twelve
years. You can ask her. Or call
around. I don't care, knowing you
will probably not make the slightest
bit of effort to verify the facts I
am presenting you.

Will you make an effort for
anything, Mr. Getty? My experience
tells me, "no". It's just much
easier to complain, isn't it? On
the off chance that you are a man of
action, may I suggest that you try
moving temporarily to a country such
as Honduras, Nicaragua, or Kenya?

These are places where medical
insurance is not a widely-known
phrase. Hell, neither is the phrase
"medical practice". And you might
find that privacy issues are
generally not given as much
consideration in these locations,
either. In fact, it isn't too
uncommon for people to find their

door being kicked down by one rebel faction or another bearing Uzis and wearing hobnailed boots for a) lodging ,b) looting, or c) just plain shits-and-giggles. And let me assure you that there are precious few insurance plans which cover those type of emergency room visits.

But you still reside in America, Mr. Getty, a bastion of freedom and choice. I would like to suggest that you take advantage of this fact. If you are truly unhappy with your insurance program, then save yourself and save your money. Quit. Simply amscray, asterd-bay. Otherwise, shut the hell up and get your whiney ass back to work.

With a big, fat, sincere fist cocked for your nose, bucko,

Earl

I have had Earl sedated and put under close observation. Cases like these upset me tremendously. It's sad, really, what the truth can do to some people.

Primitive Smites

Dear Dr. Horowitz,

Mrs. Nussbaum continues to be perturbed by the meatloaf her husband insists on preparing for dinner each new moon. I want to share a few details from our last session and see if you can give me any input, as I have been too zonked on the Prozac I've been pilfering from Nurse Amistad to come up with any ideas. She was nervous during the last session. I could tell immediately when she came into the room and crouched down behind the bookcase (a remarkable feat, considering my placement of the case and her girth), refusing to come out from it until I began ringing chimes, deluding her into the belief that the ice cream man was behind my desk.

While she riffled through my drawers (no, no, I don't mean it that way. If the case with Nurse Jones didn't convince, that thing with Clinton and Lewinsky has), I took the opportunity to ask her a few questions. I pointed out that she shouldn't be so apprehensive about her husband's preparations of meatloaf. "It's nowhere near as ominous as you make it out," I protested. "The new moon is merely coincidental. You told me yourself that you always wash all his boxers the day before he makes the meatloaf. Maybe it's just his way of celebrating."

"Listen to Doctor Wisenheimer," she snorted while shoving my engraved Cross Pen up her nose. "Means nothing, he says. Is coincidence. Then why

is he almost naked? And why all the blood?" "Mrs.
Nussbaum, he's simply draining the meat. And we've
talked many times about how your husband's pelt is so
hairy that he's been mistaken for Sasquatch many
times, even though you live in downtown
Poughkeepsie."

But she began her denial again, stating simply,
"How can you treat a supermodel like Cindy Crawford
this way? What a fucking schmuck!"

I'd appreciate your input.

Regards,

Dr. W.B. Hachenbracht

A Ray of Partly-Clouded Mentality

Dear Dr. Horowitz,

I am looking for your input on the patient I was telling you about. Ray is male, five-foot nine inches tall, one hundred sixty-four pounds, and 27 years old. He played guitar in college, football in high school and with dolls before that.

He enjoys his job as announcer at the local Piggly-Wiggly, has delusions of saving a supermodel's life on a crowded street by warning her of high cholesterol and masturbates no less than four times a day. He is, as I told you in our phone conversation, totally average in most respects.

The difference is his ego transference. He has come to see himself as a sort of *ubermensch*, and urges everyone he meets to adapt certain aspects of his personality. Below is a copy of a letter I recently received from him. I think it will give you a better idea of the seriousness of the situation. I've footnoted it to assist you with some of the references.

Dear Ray,

I was talking to Ray[2] and Ray[3] the other day, and we got to wondering about you. Specifically,

---

[2] His mother

[3] A life-sized cardboard cutout of Bob Hope

Ray[4] said, "Hey, what the hell has Ray been up to?"

We discussed the matter, and decided that your Rayness has definitely been sub-par as of late. I hate to be the one to tell you this, but if you fail to take some immediate corrective steps, we may soon no longer refer to you as Ray.

This is especially difficult for me, since I remember how you were once the Ray of Rays[5]. Remember the time we tried to do 100 nitrous oxide whippets in one evening? Neither do I, but I'll never forget that time we were sitting around doing unspeakable things to that cat with a salad fork. That dizzy chick we always made fun of came strolling in on her hands and knees and asked us why we were doing it. Then you piped up from the john and said, "They don't call me Ray for nothing." Perhaps the fact you were sitting on the thing backwards is what made it so funny, but I don't think I'll ever forget that, at least until I have another three beers.

But the fact remains that you are failing to act like the Ray of

---

[4] His mother

[5] The following anecdote is totally fictitious; it is actually a scene which was cut from the film *Animal House*.

old. Do you realize I have moved?[6]
Well then, where's my free case of
beer? Ray[7] says that this is a
sacred vow we took and the fact that
we were all naked doesn't make it
any less binding.

Sure, I realize things have
changed. Ray[8] joined Barnum Bailey
as a circus freak, but he still
sends me his skin when he's done
molting each equinox. Ray[9], who is
nearing a doctorate in graduate
school (although no one has had the
heart to tell him it is actually not
his doctorate, but William F.
Buckley's), has promised to hire me
as security when he goes on a book
tour after his thesis, *Doodles and
Scrawlings I Made During Graduate
Classes* is either published or run
through the copier a few times.
Even Ray[10], who we all used to make
fun of because he was so shy he
couldn't go to a party without
wearing his Nixon mask, has kept in

---

[6] The move was from his parent's house to a couch in the alley, and lasted only six hours.

[7] His dog, curiously enough, a large pit bull named "Lord Death"

[8] A college friend, Sam Potpie, who later died of spontaneous combustion caused by dousing himself in gasoline and repeatedly rubbing balloons on his head.

[9] I believe he is actually referring to me at this point, but his failure to mention my birthmark makes me unsure.

[10] Hans Van der Trousers, another college friend

touch by occasionally appearing at my door and punching me in the nose when I open it. I think this is our biggest disappointment in you, Ray. You are not keeping the rest of us appraised of your doings, and more importantly, whether or not you are making enough money for the rest of us to move in with you.

But there are other things as well. For instance, Ray[11] told me he has yet to receive any toenail clippings from you. And Ray[12] would like to know when you're going to finish that load of laundry he FedEx'ed you (and don't forget he likes his shirts lightly starched, and make sure you iron his handkerchiefs, and please hurry, as he's been turning his underwear inside out for almost a year now). Ray[13] told me you no longer let him stalk the women you're dating. Ray[14] complained about you canceling your subscription to his quarterly fanzine *My Favorite Smells at the Elementary School*. And your mother is either screening my calls or

---

[11] Tipper Gore. This is a misnomer. Ray had never spoken with Tipper Gore. She relayed this to him through semaphore flags.

[12] Ray's father. Again, there is exaggeration in this sentence. I had finished that laundry more than six months earlier.

[13] This may either be a self-reference, or he may mean Steven Spielburg.

[14] Definitely Steven Spielburg this time, but not the director.

hasn't been home since 1997 (plus, the bitch still owes me for the seven Grand Slam breakfasts she ate at Denny's after I covered the hotel bill).

As you can tell, your Ray performance is definitely substandard. We expect you to pick up the pace and return to your usual performance, full of Ray-ness but low in cholesterol. Ray[15], who you know is living closest to you, told me his is prepared to offer any assistance he can, from seminars to all-night drinking bouts to two-a-day minicamps to severe discipline to snuggling. Please don't let this be the last time we call you Ray.

With a Hey-Nonny-Na-and-a-Hot-Cha-Cha,

Ray

Any thoughts you have on this patient would be appreciated. Myself, I think he's one sick little boy.

Sincerely,
Dr. W.B. Hachenbracht

---

[15] A Streetlight on my block, which Ray is in the habit of calling "Ray" or sometimes, "Mr. Streetlight Who Visits Me In My Dream Land."

Yes, We Have No More Grand-mas

Dear Mr. Blickensdorfer,[16]

Meemaw[17] wore her dress inside out the whole weekend we lived at the strip club. While I know that our research will prove invaluable to future generations, I am truly beginning to fear that we can't leave her unattended anymore. Especially if we don't make sure she's locked tightly in the house before we set out.[18] Sure, the lock was secure, but apparently she gnawed through the wood flooring.

Jonsie[19] came by to check up on her, but Meemaw was gutting groundhogs and he just doesn't have the stomach for that sort of carnage. I asked her where she'd gotten the varmints, and she told me old man Potter had been shooting them in his pasture

---

[16] Mr. Blickensdorf was the name Dr. Hachenbracht used for his brother, Chris. He had trouble recalling Chris' first name, and so referred to him with his surname. This, despite the fact that Chris' parents were the same as his, and so he had the same last name as Dr. Hachenbracht.

[17] "Meemaw" is Dr. Hachenbracht's grandmother. When he was young, Dr. Hachenbracht thought that she was his great-aunt. But the passing years changed that. At the time of this writing, Dr. Hachenbracht thought that "Meemaw" was a well-preserved Eleanor Roosevelt who simply was passing herself off as family.

[18] This may sound cruel, but Dr. Hachenbracht did not literally mean that they locked their grandmother in their house. The term "house" referred to a large iron cage Hachenbracht kept in his basement, with a self-replenishing water tank.

[19] John Smith, a family friend whose name Hachenbracht also had trouble recalling.

while he sat in the barn, drinking Canadian Mist out of a jelly jar. He only quits when he runs out of ammo or gets too drunk to see straight[20]. My mom always told me that he wasn't ever the same after he got back from the Big One. Seeing the Red Sox drop the World Series like that just broke his heart, and when he returned he just didn't have the heart to continue his Oliver Hardy impressions[21].

I'm just sorry you couldn't be here for that gopher stew. Damn, it was good. Meemaw may not be as sharp as she once was, but she still can cook a varmint, even if she does it with her dress on inside out. It calms her down, too[22]. She wouldn't be able to function in an old folk's home unless they let her work in the cafeteria. While she was buttering the biscuits, she told me that story about her and Lottie going to Memphis to meet Elvis, and how Lottie left a trail of typhus cases at every public swimming pool they stopped at, and how they got so hungry after spending the night at the depot, smelling bus fumes, that they got up early and sneaked into a farmer's barn and ate nearly half a bale of hay...the good stuff, too, almost pure alfalfa, no Timothy grass hardly at all.[23]

---

[20] This is a joke, as Potter was perpetually cross-eyed.

[21] Potter was a phenomenal impressionist who once was able to extort a considerable amount of money from the Kellogg cereal company before they realized he was not actually Count Dracula.

[22] Dr. Hachenbracht's grandmother once 'calmed down' so much while preparing wildlife that she was almost buried as a result. It was only when the priest attempted to pry the knife and chopping block from her hands before burial that she returned to her senses and asked for another Singapore Sling.

[23] This story was legendary in the Hachenbracht family. Unfortunately, it has no historical basis. Dr. Hachenbracht's grandmother was actually going to see Harvey Corman.

She's doing well since then, only took her clothes off at the mailbox once, and hasn't set fire to anything in the shed at all. Just wanted you to know that she wore her dress inside out, though. It seemed rather important.[24]

Best,

Dr. W.B. Hachenbracht

---

[24] His grandmother ceased the practice of wearing clothes inside out shortly after this letter, choosing instead to wear lacy undergarments which showed off her midriff – a look which Madonna later admitted influenced her early clothing choices.

Career Opportunities, Strife Decisions

Dear Henry[25],

The boll weevils are turning up in the attic again[26]. Sadly, this time around they've gotten hold of your favorite varsity jacket[27], the one from the water-boy at Nantucket High, who could get a cup of Gatorade © to the huddle faster than Carl Lewis and was hung like a horse on top of it.

It was sad that he left you at the altar like that[28], but the fact that you insisted on growing dreadlocks for the wedding was probably a big factor. After all, nobody wanted to tell you this at the time, but you reeked of reefer and mosquito repellent during the rehearsal dinner. Well, it's not the first time your love of marijuana and your fear of malaria have cost you, is it[29]?

---

[25] A boyhood friend who became a farrier, only to quit when he discovered that he would have to work with horses. It bothered him enough to undergo a sex change. At the time of this writing, she was doing odd jobs as a handyman and even ones as a waitress.

[26] This is a code phrase Dr. Hachenbracht used to let others know it was baseball season. In this situation, though, it refers to some boll weevils, which had found their way into his attic.

[27] It was actually Dr. Hachenbracht's favorite jackets, which explains why it was in his attic in the first place.

[28] The phrase "like that" referred to a bat out of hell.

[29] Henry had also lost a 1984 Nissan Centra after she, under the influence of marijuana, drove it through a puddle which she was convinced was infested with mosquito larva and abandoned it in front of a Krispy Kreme store.

It's time to face facts. You can't live in the past. In fact, it's time you quit living in that factory[30]. They all know you don't work there, and the coffee you make is godawful. You're varsity jacket is gone. So are your looks, and the Chief Wahoo head you had stuck in the yard (vandals, we're guessing, but we're waiting to see if a ransom note shows up[31]). There's a vacancy at the cannery, and salmon season is due to start either at the next full moon or when LuEllen quits menstruating (yes, the EPA has been hounding her about that, but old habits die hard). Let me know if you're interested[32].

Sincerely,

Dr. W.B. Hachenbracht

---

[30] Hirschfield's Liniment and Old-Fashioned Salve Corporation

[31] None ever did, although Dr. Hachenbracht did receive a very nice catalogue from the Fingerhut Corporation the very next day.

[32] Henry instead chose to pursue a career betting on the ponies in Lexington, Kentucky. Unfortunately, her choice proved deadly when she failed to realize the track was for the horses only and she was trampled to death in the first heat.

Some Like You Hot

Dear Mr. Malley,

Your letter came to my attention today. My patient, "S", brought it to me, complaining of nausea. "This bastard makes me sick! Sick, sick, sick!" he screamed before trying to insert his tongue into a fax machine in my office. "You save on long distance charges this way," he explained.

I realize that S is going through some difficult transitions right now. Although he is a man of letters, especially the vowels and sometimes "Y", he has, under my advice, foresworn returning missives until he can recall what "WYSIWYG" means and can create a new definition for "QWERTY".

But to assuage any fears you may have, I have taken the liberty of mailing you a letter explaining S's current state.

The truth of the matter is that S has had something of a breakdown. To put it in a metaphor you might grasp more readily, it is not so much a matter of overhauling his psyche as it is installing a new muffler. Luckily, I was able to fit him into my schedule and he was able to mortgage his house, thus affording my services.

Under my expert analysis, I have discovered two existing afflictions in S, and given some time, may be able to encourage a third. Firstly, S suffers from a rare type of reverse narcissus complex. I hope to name this disorder after myself, or failing that, my dog. S has fallen in love with an image, but it isn't his and, thus, is someone else's.

Namely, Mr. Malley, it is you. After S received several letters from you, he said the scales fell from his eyes (which he was measuring at the time) and he realized you were living the perfect life, at least in comparison to his. While he slaves over the keys of his computer, trying to compose a list of Life's secrecy, you slave over your secretaries, trying to compose a list that will push all their keys.

S also suffers from the more common dysfunction of agoranecroxenolupophiliaphobia, or fear of being sodomized by a dead, non-indigenous wolf in public.

The treatment of such warped perceptions is understandably tricky, and I immediately began to charge more for each session. We then administered several session of shock treatment by sticking S's forefinger into a light socket.

I then began using sensory deprivation techniques, where I would blindfold him and expose him to his fear, telling him as I slowly walked towards him: "I'm a big wolf. Oh-ho, I'm a big wolf, all right, and I'm bad too. Yes, I'm a big, bad, baaad wolf. And boy, am I horny. But what I can I do about that? I mean, I'm very big, and I'm very bad, but I'm walking around here in this department store. And I couldn't do anyone here, in front of all these people, could I? But maybe I could. After all, I'm a very, very, big wolf and I'm very, very bad, and I'm not even from this country." When S would burst into tears, I would comfort him by licking his scalp.

S has also begun rehabilitative therapy which I hope will allow him to write once more, or, at the very least, join some chimpanzees I have in the laboratory who have shown great promise in reconstructing *Hamlet*, with the character Horatio rewritten to suit Arnold Shwartzennegger's taste. I have been stuffing his ears with hot dogs and then sitting before a computer, working it in such a manner as to suggest that I was editing the newest edition of *The New Yorker*. When S began to masturbate, I would quickly have an assistant remove the hotdogs so he could hear that I was actually using the keys of a piano. He would soon calm down and join me on spoons for our rendition of "The Entertainer".

I have kept S on a strict diet of eggs, bacon and psyllicybum. True, this makes him delusional, but the cholesterol keeps him logy enough to prevent any mishaps. Besides, he's a hell of a lot more fun this way. S has expressed a strong desire to improve himself by hiding in a cardboard box and dousing himself with real Vermont maple syrup.

He has made great improvements and can now answer a ringing telephone without shouting, "Bastard! No onions! No onions!! Extra cheese, you shit!" but now inquires, "You Laverne?"

I hope you find this report as inspiring as I find the possibilities of getting a book deal for this case. S sends his regards and some navel lint, which you will find enclosed.

Sincerely,

Dr. W.B. Hachenbracht

Beer and Loathing

Dear Dr. Horowitz,

    I hope this letter finds you rolling in clover, or at least rubbing some alfalfa grass on your knees. I am positive this little horticulture kick of yours will soon pass, but I begrudge you none of the pleasures you claim to experience living on the lean ribs of the land.

    However, I hope you are able to kick off your clod-hoppers long enough to give me some suggestions for my newest patient. "Miguel" is a professional journalist whose increasing paranoia over the past few years has been matched only by his intake of illicit drugs. He was recently discovered in an East Texas coastal town, where he had been living on an abandoned oil well which he claimed was "the renowned Unkie Sol's, you fascist swine!" He had been missing for nearly a month, and the only clues to his whereabouts during that time were a packet of letters found in pressboard briefcase which had been soaked with blotter acid. I have enclosed the originals for your perusal, but I suggest you wear a pair of gloves before examining them. My receptionist fell asleep with her forehead on them during her after-lunch nap and spent the next seventeen hours staring at light fixtures, which she described as "groovy," and addressing me as "Mr. Sulu".

Dear Mr. Von Rollolostein,

Your toadies showed up as scheduled, but Jonah didn't think that it was proper for me to demand to replace the hood ornament of his Jaguar with my glow-in-the-dark statuette of Elvis. So I decided to teach him a bit of a lesson. Rather than provide table service, which we will no doubt need in your mountain hideaway (you never think of such civilized touches...probably thought it would be just fine for us to eat caviar off paper plates, old tuna cans, etc.), I slipped on some brass knuckles and gave their canines a thorough massage.

I left them propped up against that toilet in my front yard (which Doc Circumference has YET to pick up from the bachelor party, by the way), slipped a *I'm With Stupid* T-shirt over Jonah and shaved his eyebrows and took off.

I've got enough crystal meth to get me to the Sierra Nevadas, and my Alf doll if shoved down my pants to impress the ladies. But until you wire me with money and directions, I'm just going to head south. You can reach me via e-mail or at Unkie Solomon's Good Tyme Eatery and Wet Bar in Mobile, AL

Sincerely,

Miguel Duke

Honorable Lichtenstien (nee Duke),

My advice is stay put, be it Alabama, be it Idaho, be it Mexico City.

As you may have heard, likely through that rat-fink Anders "Mother-Lover" Jones, the mountain hideaway was made all too public in a very unfortunate DEA raid. All were taken. We fear the worst for Dr. Circumference, though unsubstantiated reports claim our reported Professor disappeared into a mysteriously large crowd, disguised as a woman, driving a mini-clown car.

Though we all know his love of tequila, not mention his obsession with sheer, low-cut, strapless dresses (nor his fancy for lace undies and the backseats of small, foreign cars), the fact remains that his dogs were left unfed, and the commanding DEA officer's face was lipstick-smeared and smiling. Until further notice I've taken a job at the 7-11 on highway 54, Bellevue, Illinois. Should you need my assistance, write your request on a note, place that note in a plastic bag, and send it to me in a bottle of whiskey. Your answer will come on the inside of a Bazooka Joe gum wrapper, sent via Clown Courier. Times like these require the utmost caution, not to mention lots of whiskey.

A Bird In the Hand Squeals Like a Pig in Heat,

Baron Roland Von Rollolostein

Senor Von Rollolostein,

I have some good news, finally, in the midst of this debacle. Dr. Circumference has shown up at Unkie Solomon's (Mssr. Bastido to his friends), and the DEA bust will come to naught, because the dear ol' Prof. has stuffed an absolutely amazing amount of acid and ganja into his vehicle.

We have sent the local pizzeria in the mountains a check for $6,000 and instructed them to deliver four pies a day (two pepperoni, one sausage and one with The Works) to the hideaway, as well as make sure the bathtub is kept full, until further notice.

This should keep the dogs happy, as well as any feds who might be lingering about the scene, taking in the scenery while they bake the last batch of marijuana brownies Jonah had placed in the freezer.

Doc is happy to be in the south, and has started to get a real following her at Unkie S's (Thursday's are now drag night). Unfortunately, he didn't bring any extra gowns besides the strapless sequin number (you know the one: captivated the prince during last

year's Halloween festivities in St.
Louis). Please send whatever you
can spare from your closet, or see
if Ned has any. Doc C thinks he
stole a few from him when they went
on their last drinking binge.

Humming a Hum Which Actually
Has Words,

Miguel Duke

Doctor Duke,

I don't mean to alarm you, but the most
recent clown courier to drop off a case of Old
Crow up here turned out to be none other than
the venerable (perhaps you say "distinguished")
Dr. Circumference himself.

He claims to have no knowledge of Unkie
Sol's, nor of your ex-wife's extensive collection of
negligées that disappeared two years ago. He
offers a story of escape that matches those of the
witnesses tortured on his behalf, a story of
intrigue, underwater labyrinths and disfigured
though simultaneously stunning women, of hot
dog stands and leech-infested swamps. Though
I am sure he is lying about the underwear, his
eyes, though behind a flood of tears and pound
of mascara, told me he was honest in regards to
both his escape from the mountain compound
and Unkie Sol's.

Though he was encouraged to hear about
the drag night and his supposed sexual exploits
with the honorable Judge Wallawallawallawoop,

he was concerned and I now fear that an imposter is on the loose.

Possibly DEA, but we can't be sure as he might be ATF, NRA, NEA, or perhaps DUI. At the same time, I fear that this Doctor may be the false of the two. And there is the possibility, thought terrifying it may be, that both Dr. Circumferences are imposters. Please advise on future action. To be safe, send false documents via clown courier, and true by bottle rocket. Make it the whistling kind so I know it's from you.

Yours in a tub of peanut butter and midgets,

Baron Roland Von Rollolostein

Herr   Unterhunde   Von Rollolostein,

It is a dark day when our enemies turn to such clandestine methods to upset our plans. I regret to inform you the Dr. Circumference is NO DOUBT an imposter, as the real good doctor is currently massaging my midsection as I type this on an old Army-issued keyboard and a 256 MG computer made of erector sets and some old floppy disks and various pieces of a 1974 Ford Fairline.

The one who delivered my last message to you is probably on the pay of the DEA or ATF, arriving DUI from BFE via the QEW. I recommend you take proper action so that he may be pronounced DOA ASAP.

It is the only plan of action, which will prevent things from becoming FUBAR in the near future. Should you doubt my message (which, I apologize in advance, will be delivered by Roman Candle, rather than bottle rocket – it's all Nervous Charlie had, what with the Labor Day rush on fireworks and all), I advise you to disregard this clown's story of escape. No doubt he picked it up from my recent biography: *Terror in My Pants: A Story of Intrigue, Underwater Labyrinths and Disfigured Though Simultaneously Stunning Women, of Hot Dog Stands and Leech-Infested Swamps and How to Beat a Bearish Stock Market.* It was at number 19 on the New York Times bestseller list last week.

Slap-Happily,

Miguel Duke

As you can tell, Dr. H., there is a dreadful disconnection with reality, as well as psychosis which threatens violence at all times. All attempts to locate this Baron Von Rollolostein have been completely unsuccessful. We are not sure if he is a *nome de plum*, or simply someone who may not actually be named Baron Von Rollolostein.

One thing is certain. Miguel is an ugly character, and perhaps may be one of the most disconnected, drug-addled people I've met in my many years of psychotherapy. So, what do you think? Should I charge double?

Sincerely,

Dr. W.B. Hachenbracht

Studies and Musings

Physician, Humor Thyself

Laughter may, after all, be the best medicine to cure the woes of everyday life. There are dozens of documented cases of terminally ill people recovering after experiencing more than their share of belly laughs.

A woman suffering from a sever case of hemorrhoids in Wichita, Kansas, recovered sufficiently to realize her dream of streaking during the 1989 Academy Awards after she was allowed to repeatedly view her husband attempting to aerobicize.

A man in Youngstown, Ohio, was stricken with a mysterious paralysis that doctors were unable to explain or cure. The man remained an invalid for two years, until his wife received such a ridiculous haircut that he laughed to the point of tears for two hours and suddenly recovered the use of his hands, which, ironically, had been amputated almost a year before.

Perhaps the most touching story is that of a young boy who, suffering from an unknown disease, had been forced to spend his entire life at Disneyland. But after he viewed an HBO def comedy jam special, he suddenly became well enough to fulfill his dream of spending a week at a Ronald McDonald House.

Pondering cases such as these, the power of comedy is difficulty to deny, although there are some detractors who might suggest that it is still easy to mispronounce. I have strove to explain and understand comedy ever since I discovered that I could make funny noises by placing my hand in my armpit and squeezing. Although this has given me only four months to study my subject, I believe that I have come to understand the workings of humor sufficiently to set forth a rough outlining of the mechanics of comedy.

First of all, it is important to understand comedy as an entity capable of standing on its own, and not, for example, as a pizza topping. Thus, our question becomes "How can humor survive without topicalities?" rather than, "Can I have extra cheese on that, please?"

Comedy can, of course, derive much from current subjects, and in fact much laughter has derived from topical snafus, as well as the never-ending fact that men look extremely funny when they masturbate. But comedy can often rely on its own mechanical workings for successful results. In order to understand the nature of comedy, we must first examine its workings, as well as quit thinking of fart jokes as the zenith of humor.

One of the first things that may be said of the workings of humor is that it is rarely repetitious. A worthwhile note to make while on this subject is that humor is rarely repetitious. Thus, we see that there is no need to reiterate a point to in hopes of getting more humor from it. For example the punchline, "Ronald Reagan was acting like a complete moron during the Iran-Contra hearings" would be far more succinct if it were worded simply, "Ronald Reagan."

A finger could be pointed at many sources of humor, but it should never be pointed at one's own buttocks while in Canada, since this gesture translates as meaning, "Representational of your ancestors." In fact, many comedians have split over the concept of 'logic drawn to absurdism,' versus the concept of 'bodily functions explained in detail'.

Groups of experts have set out to explore both concepts. Unfortunately, they were sidetracked at a local pub and, although they were discovered laughing hysterically at the time, they were unable to explain what so damn funny when they sobered up.

Another point to make on the working of humor concerns the use of making a 'play on words'. This use of wordplay is best illustrated in the following parable:

A young man went to see his guidance counselor one day and said, "Sir, I am not happy with my classes at college. They often seem rhetorical and boring to me." The guidance counselor replied, "Why are you worrying about that? What about when you graduate and you can't find a job? Now there's something to worry about. Don't be a schmuck." "But, sir," the young persisted, "Don't my studies affect the kind of job I will look for later?" The guidance counselor pointed a finger at his buttocks. "Representational of your ancestors," he replied coldly.

What can we learn from this? The word play in this anecdote is the key to the humor in it, but it is also very subtle. The word play of the joke exists in two separate but interrelated roles.

First of all, during the entire conversation, the student is attempting to complete a crossword puzzle, but is unable to solve 49 down, "Impending darkness, i.e., like a cave." The answer, of course, being "cave-ish".

The second part of the word play springs from the fact that the instructor is not a Canadian at all, but has descended from Irish bloodlines. Thus, his use of a Canadian is put-down is completely inappropriate, yet far more humorous than the traditional Irish insult of, "Fuck you, Mr. Potatohead." Combining these two factors gives the parable its exhilarating freshness, along with a touch of irreverent nihilism.

Having stated that humor is not repetitious and pointed out the importance of word plays, we now turn to the all-important aspect of delivery. Delivery refers to the timing of the joke, and while it rather a complex subject, we can compare it to the delivery of a pizza with mushrooms and black olives.

First of all, we must dial the number of the pizza parlor, which is analogous to preparing the joke. If you are unsure of the joke you want to tell, simply check in the yellow pages under "J".

Now comes the actual ordering of the pizza for delivery, or simply, the "delivery," in comedy terms. When the pizza delivery people ask if they can help you, ask if they have Prince Albert in a can. If they say yes, order them to release him at once. If they say no, then…oh, I don't know…giggle like a maniac and ask them what they would like on their pizza. Most people who answer phones at pizza places are only slightly more perceptive than the average steel-belted tire anyhow.

The factors that operate in the workings of humor are far too numerous for me to list or count, even with my shoes and socks off. But with the fundamentals listed here, almost anyone will be able to publish one of their jokes in *Reader's Digest*.

One of the best summaries on humor I have ever heard came from a stranger I met while vacationing in Detroit. He said, "What may be funny to one person may strike another as dumb, pathetic, or even offensive. But you can always get a laugh by pulling someone's pants down." Then he punched me in the nose and took my wallet. I only hope that everyone has a chance to learn such a valuable lesson.

Among the Tattoo People of East-Central Ohio

The area of America referred to as Ohio has several larger cities, well-known for their spectacular rust designs which are created by building large buildings in the downtown area and then moving out of them. These areas have been the subjects of countless anthropological studies. Little documentation, however, has been made of the less-populated towns, which dot the landscape in between the metropolises.

Perhaps the most interesting of these smaller towns are the subcultures that originate within them. While larger cities support a vast array of soci-economic classes, smaller towns tend to divide themselves into two basic categories: those who have, and those who just have tattoos.

Those of the tattooed persuasion are a little-studied phenomenon, mostly due to their penchant for rough behavior, such as using shotguns during domestic disputes, and the hours they keep. What follows is one of the first exhaustive studies made on these tattooed people of east central Ohio. Much of the information which follows has been extensively researched and documented by copying entire pages out of the *Encyclopedia Britannica*.

These people are difficult to communicate with, being a reticent lot who view documentation of their ways with suspicion and also have a tendency to speak without opening their mouths. However, using the time-honored traditions of Buying The Next Round, I was able to gain their confidence and over a period of time (at least five weeks, to the best of my recollection) I meticulously gathered the information for this first anthropological study of one of the strongest sub-cultures in the Midwest: The Tattoo People of East Central Ohio.

Definitions:

In order to specifically buttonhole the subjects of this study and, more importantly, to make this paper appear to be the work of an academic, the following definitions must be used to better understand the exact class of people this study examines.

Tattoo – Defined as the distinct markings the people use to identify themselves to each other. These marks are indelible ink portraits usually appearing on the forearm or biceps of the subject. Popular items include eagles, snakes, wolves and occasionally, self-portraits. Phrases are often used in combination with, or independent of, a picture tattoo, depending on whether there is one to accompany it or not. Phrases tend to vary a great deal, as they reflect the subjects' personality more acutely. They run the gamut from "MOTHER" to "I can read all by myself". It is also useful to employ Webster's definition of tattoo as "to beat or rap rhythmically on," since the tattoo people will often use their fists to apply such a definition to an outsider's face as punishment for a cultural faux pas, such as looking at them.

People – While many factors are usually used in determining the scientific classification of the species Homo sapiens, these factors are often ignored by the tattoo people, especially those concerning cognitive abilities and the use of silverware while dining. Thus, "people" are hereby defined for this study as "omnivorous mammals using bi-pedality or a Chevy truck for locomotion."

East Central Ohio – Those areas not being north, south or west, generally located somewhere between Cleveland and Columbus. This may also be referred to as "Bum-Fuck Egypt". Take your pick.

Tattoos:

Having already defined what constitutes a tattoo, it is interesting to look at how these decorations are applied and used, although not as interesting as looking at a shapely next-door-neighbor undressing after she has forgotten to pull down the blind.

The tattoos are generally placed in places where they are conspicuous in normal dress clothing. Thus, their placement is usually on the arm of the men and the calf of the women, or occasionally, the midriff.

The tattoo serves as an identifying mark for the group. They are received voluntarily by each individual who is usually so eager to receive his mark that he may not even have a specific pattern in mind, at least until he sobers up the next morning. With a tattoo, the members of the culture are able to express their individuality and machismo, as well as do neat tricks when they flex their muscles. By providing such obvious group identification, the tattoo people are able to quickly recognize each other in larger gatherings. This serves to facilitate their social interactions, such as courting, establishing unofficial leadership and forming heavy-metal bands.

Language:

The tattoo people speak a dialect of the Standard English language. One of the major impediments in speaking with this group is the fact that they rarely take the time to move their mouths while speaking. People suffering from lockjaw have been mistaken for members of the tattoo people culture in the past.

Before attempting to interact with people of this culture, it is advisable to study up on any available knowledge of firearms, gunracks and motor vehicles, since these subjects tend to pepper the majority of any tattoo person's conversation. Other subjects which the group tends to study in detail include: alcohol, fights, T & A and professionals of all kinds, usually referred to as "Those Fuckers" (e.g. "Those Fuckers told me that I could keep the car, but my old lady got possession of the house.")

When engaging in conversations with a member of this culture, always try to bear in mind this axiom: "Obscenities are in...articulation ain't."

Work:

They hate it.

And for good reason. Because they usually man the dullest assembly-line-type occupations to be had. This is due mostly to the fact that most tattoo people are slightly less perceptive and creative than the average crow bar. Those members with a bit more ingenuity have figured out how to make the welfare system work for them.

Those who haven't stay with what they have, in order to afford their social habits. Thus, the popular corruption of the old adage, "Work is the curse of the drinking class." Well, not that you'd ever hear most of these people use such a term. Most of them think that 'adage' is the opposite of subtraction. But you get the idea.

Social Patterns:

Most of the tattoo people tend to define their time into two different periods: "their time" and "my time". Or, phrased more simply, sober and drunk. The reason time spent sober is defined as "their time" is that it is spent at the workplace, where people see themselves as indentured to their employers. Of course, as in any other case, there are exceptions to this rule of sobriety at the workplace. Such exceptions usually lead to a form of cultural entertainment known as "industrial accidents."

As a culture, the people tend group together in virtually all situations. The rare exception is hunting trips, when the men will fan out over a large wooded area in order to mistake each other as deer. Despite the uniformity of their culture, socio-economic positioning, values and the gas mileage of their trucks, the tattoo people constantly manage to find things to dispute during the large amounts of time they spend in each other's company. These disputes usually center on more subjective values, such as whether or not one member may be "a complete dickhead" or not. If the member is found to measure poorly against such criteria, he is subject to a wide range of punishments, ranging from being the butt of jokes to being ignored while his friends join in sexually-harassing a woman. Which brings us to our next category of study...

Rituals:

As with most cultures, the tattoo people have many shared activities that they engage in with enough regularity to consider them rituals of social behavior. As we have mentioned above, harassing women is one of those activities. Here, we should make note of the fact most of the rituals are divided into two basic categories: what the men do and what the women do.

Sexism is the basis for who performs which ritual. Men are primarily responsible for working for income, while women are responsible for cooking, cleaning, child rearing and working for an income.

This division is reflected in the rituals of the tattoo people as well. For instance, sexual harassment is an activity engaged in almost exclusively by men, while it is an activity enjoyed almost exclusively by women. The reason for this is that harassment is as near to a complement as most tattoo men are willing to get. They are somewhat reserved with their complements, preferring to save them for their trucks and guns.

Most notable of the tattoo people's rituals is their habit of incorporating their motor vehicles into their courting routines. The culture respects the ability to drive so much that it is often relied upon when the necessary motor skills for walking have ceased to exist after last call. Hence, driving a car is a crucial part of winning a woman's heart. It is used to draw her attention in the early stages of romance, woo her feelings later with the use of the back seat, escort her proudly in public during the heady initial days of the romance and finally, to chase her down the street as a sign of the close of the relationship.

Home:

For the tattoo people, the popular saying would be best expressed, "Home is where the car keys are." For there is very little reason for them to visit it otherwise.

Families of the tattoo people tend to be very close in age across generations. It is not uncommon to meet a great grandmother under the age of sixty. It is less uncommon to find a great grandmother under the influence.

This combination of liquor consumption and closely-aged generations results in a volatile mixture at best. Add to this the fact that father is rarely present and sometimes known only by paternity blood tests, and you get a short-tempered, hormone-powered matriarchy. This is the basic familial structure for an average clan of tattooed people. And brother, you don't want to visit it on a full-moon night after the local Kroger's has run a special on Busch Light.

The basic structure of the actual home of a family of tattooed people usually runs in the trailer variety, from the woebegone singlewide to the luxurious, basemented double. All of these homes seem to share a few peculiar similarities, no matter the status of the occupant, be it McDonald's grill cook to Wendy's Nightshift Manager. First of all, they all tend to produce little in the way of comely botanical growth. That is to say, all their lawns are inevitably dead or well on their way to it. Perhaps this is due to the unceasing waterings provided by rampaging toddlers who wander the grounds of the trailer after slipping the confining bonds of their diapers. Perhaps the septic tank was buried too deeply, denying the grass roots precious water and E-Coli nutrients. Either way, the shrubs somehow manage to thrive, obscuring mailboxes, windows, and, if left unattended long enough, the trailer itself. Perhaps there is a method to the madness of the tattooed people's lawn-care rituals.

A quick breakdown of the family hierarchy should be mentioned in relation to the home. The easiest to discuss are all those falling under the category of 'teenagers' or 'men of the house.' These two social phenomenon often fall within the same grouping. They can be recognized by their surly behavior, their unwillingness to deal with the women of the house, and the long tire skid marks they left when they burned out of the driveway.

After this category come the women of the house, who are the ones who have most recently added new life to the ranks of the family. They are a quiet lot, unless they are awake, and especially if they have been awakened by the squealing of tires pulling out of the driveway.

Assisting these women are various grandmothers and aunts, varying in number depending on whether this is the first, third or seventh marriage, and whether any of those marriages took place in Las Vegas.

There are also various men in this age category (14 years to cheating death), but they have already left with the asshole who burned out of the garage.

Then come the elders of the family. Their wisdom has been gained by fighting in at least three of the two world wars, voting for prohibition, assisting bootleggers, serving at least one jail term, living in a commune, refusing to "join in all that hippie bullshit", making several fortunes, losing them to various vices and charitable causes. All this wisdom is spewed out in various forms at various times in return for a) getting' me another beer, my dearie, b) scratchin' grampie's phantom toes, or c) shuttin' the hell up for five seconds. The elders of the family also enjoy executive privileges, deciding what should be cooked for dinner, who has to sleep on the couch tonight and whose bail will be paid come Saturday morning.

Finally, there are the youngest members of this conflagration, the babes and toddlers who will one day ascend to the crown position of their elders.

These progeny seem to exhibit only three emotions: crying; eating; sleeping. It leads this investigator to the conclusion they are either trying to tuck away enough energy to decry their slated roles, or are preparing for their future incarcerations long ahead of time.

<u>Conclusions:</u>

It's their world. And they can have it.

Chapter II (Prologue)

The area surrounding the Ohio River is mostly hilly, except where it is somewhat flatter. These hills were once the size of mountains, but through erosion from the elements, or a very successful diet, they were reduced greatly in size. Which was good, because in their original state, they were nearly impassable, even with a four-wheel-drive vehicle. Not that there were such things as cars back then, but you get the idea.

All wildlife was indigenous, except for that which arrived by rail. But that was nearly two and a half millennia later, and is of no concern for our study. Deer abounded, and many wolves abounded after them, and in a much quicker fashion, for the deer was a staple of the wolves' diet. Well, let's not pull any punches. If the wolves couldn't have caught any deer, they would've been between a rock and a hard place that sounds like 'famine'.

A balance was struck between the animals in the area. Nature was in accord, and all of the earth seemed to be shaking its groove thing. Except for the crawdads, who were indignant at finding themselves at the bottom of the food chain.

Native Americans began showing up in the area around 800 BC. This was a little earlier than most people thought they should be arriving, but this aboriginal culture had no words that translated as "stylishly late." In fact, they had few words that translated into much at all. Most of their words had to do with deer, which was the staple of their existence, providing food and clothing, but it made them very dull conversationalist at parties.

Water, while used in their diet, had never been such a big thing in their lives before. They quickly adapted to the area near the river, adding such words as "swimming", "drowning" and "skinny-dipping" to their vocabulary.

In time, these gentle people began to think of the river as a provider, and also a dictator. The river would provide fish and game for the tribes who lived next to it. But the waters could also rise, and create great destruction. Some Native Americans began to think of her as a strong mother, providing bounty equally, but also determined to protect what was rightly hers. Others as more of a sleepy squaw, who might not notice a few quick moves, but could give you a kick between the legs that would send you reeling if you got too frisky.

The Native Americans began living a life of harmony with the rivers. They fished her waters. Boated on her currents in bark canoes. Ate funny-looking mushrooms and stared at the moving water for hours at a time. They hunted the animals which came to the river to drink, and sipped from the muddy banks themselves. But only once or twice: the cramping and quick runs to the woods taught all the Indians the value of spring water.

Then came the White Man. Some of the earliest white settlers in the area were German Socialists who hoped to form great communal villages near the river. They kicked native tribes off the property and built their own village there, which pissed the original occupants off to no end, since they were already living a communal lifestyle and felt these Krauts were ripping off their idea.

The Native Americans talked of revenge, of raids, fires, and t.p.-ings. Their peaceable nature, and the lack of toilet paper, prevailed in the end, and they moved away from the Germans to quieter places along the river valley.

But even these were beginning to have their share of visitors from Europe. Eventually, the Indians began hanging out with French fur traders, partially because the Frenchmen were more sympathetic to their cause and worked well with their bartering system, but mostly because they were party guys who always had plenty of firewater. In fact, some Native American tribes hit the bottle so hard that they agreed to sign almost every piece of paper placed in front of them. They were so soused that the hangover has persisted through generations, right up to today, although most tribes prefer to use the word "reservation". Still, you can give these original Americans credit, since they never picked up that disgusting habit of eating frog legs.

Reflections on a Mirror

What can we say about a mirror? A lot, I suppose, but how much would we repeat in front of our parents?

Mirrors are interesting phenomena. Man has striven for a way to view himself as others do ever since he realized turning very quickly just wasn't going to do it.

As a psychiatrist, mirrors serve as an interesting subject for me. Some people see mirrors as simply a way to make sure the part in their hair is all right. I find them almost mystic, an allegory of another side our personality.

But mirrors are a different matter completely. I remember one subject who was convinced he saw a deadly assassin from the future each time he looked in the mirror. After nearly two years of counseling, I convinced him it was merely his own reflected image, but in need of a shave.

A mirror represents an interesting physical manifestation; sure, it looks like our image in that thing, but why are we using the other hand to snip those nose hairs? It's a strange image, a reversal of everything we know and accept, and nothing to think about for too long when you have to sleep by yourself in a house that creaks.

Why does the image use the "wrong" hand to tackle the problem we present it? Maybe the image is a parallel of our universe. Perhaps we're blocking the light using the hand we do. Either way, we're not going to find out by staring at ourselves while sitting on the toilet.

We need to consider the mirror as an allegorical medium, rather than a true physical representation of our lives. This doesn't mean that it isn't fun to make faces at yourself, though. As a matter of fact, Thomas Edison often thought he could see if a good idea was forming by tilting his head back far enough to peer up his nostrils.

Reflections are a necessary part of our lives, in every aspect. We must take stock of ourselves periodically, review our progress and errors, examine our emotional well being, peer at our spiritual growth and make sure there are no boogers clinging to our mustaches.

In short, we ought to use a mirror at all points of our lives, no matter what we are trying to discover about ourselves. I recall one patient who felt he was under tremendous pressure, hounded by forces from all aspects of his life: family, work, secret society clubs, phone solicitors, friends, a certain gorilla at the primate display at the San Francisco zoo. I encouraged him to reflect on the patterns he had developed in dealing with stress. After some intense self-reflection, he happened to look up from the *Mad* magazine he was reading and saw in the mirror that one of his practical-joke-loving friends had dropped an anvil on his head several weeks before, causing his neck to collapse into his shoulders. After some corrective surgery and several more therapy sessions, my patient felt well enough to approach his friend and slash his face with a broken bottle.

We all need to assess our progress. We all need to stare at ourselves in the mirror, no matter what type of reflection we're seeking. But not when we're naked or someone is watching. That's just asking for trouble.

The legend of Narcissus is he fell in love with his own reflection and wouldn't budge from the water, which provided the image he so worshipped. As a result, he not only missed dinner that night, but they eventually had to build the mall around him and had to eliminate the space where the Starbucks would've gone. But is that so wrong? We all need to look in the mirror at some point and ask ourselves the same question: is that a blackhead coming on, or just some melanoma?

ISBN 155212373-1